Lugged Bicycle Frame Construction: A Manual

Build a bicycle frame with a $35 torch and other inexpensive tools

Marc-Andre R. Chimonas

Text and Photographs, Copyright 2009 Marc Chimonas

Authors note: If the print quality of the photographs in this manuscript is either too light or too dark to give useful information, please complain to the entity from where the book was purchased.

Table of Contents

Chapter 1: Introduction

Forward

As a medical student, I was always short on cash. I rode single track with a $360 mountain bike, and paying someone else for maintenance was out of the question. I taught myself how to tweak derailleurs and brakes through trial and error. I gradually accumulated bicycle specific tools and learned to service headsets, bottom brackets, cones, and true a wheel. Eventually I build up my skill set to the point where I could strip down and build up a frameset and tear down and rebuild a suspension fork.

By the time I decided to attempt frame building, I had solidified my sense of independence and self reliance. Good hands on frame building courses were available, but they were pricy, lengthy, and far away. Furthermore, I was determined to teach myself rather than have someone guide me through the whole process. In retrospect, this decision was a mistake.

My father-in-law gave me a brief, one-hour brazing lesson at his farm. Although he knew little about bicycles, the experience was invaluable. Despite this lesson, building my first bicycle frame was an incredibly frustrating process. It took me well over 100 hours. I did everything wrong the first time around and repeatedly had to tear apart and re-braze my subassemblies. Essentially, I built two bicycles even though I had only one frameset to show for my efforts. I bought tools I didn't need, and I often bought the wrong size steel tubing. In the end, I wasted much time and spent two to three times the money that was necessary. The resulting frame, although sturdy, was pretty ugly.

Part of the problem I experienced was the lack of a single, concise, entry-level manual. There were excellent resources out there both in print and on the internet. However, I often felt overwhelmed and had trouble figuring out which techniques would work well for the frame I wanted to build and which would work well for other frames. I also didn't know what techniques would work well for my meager collection of tools or my mechanical skill set. The bike I intended to build, a fillet-brazed mountain bike, was a bit too ambitious of a goal for a first time builder working on his own.

The purpose of this manual is to provide a basic, theoretical foundation and a step-by-step walkthrough for the first time frame builder. This manual is not a comprehensive guide to bicycle frame building. That manual had already been written, *The Paterek Manual For Bicycle Framebuilders,* and is an excellent reference. However, the numerous techniques and 500+ pages can be a bit daunting to the first time builder. The manual I have written presents the first time builder with step-by-step plans to build his first bicycle frame.

4

What We Cover in This Manual

Bicycle frame building is both a science and an art. Building a bicycle frame out of 4 pounds (lbs) of steel, which does not break under the weight of a 200 lbs rider, is a science. Making that same frame aesthetically pleasing with elegant lines and clever color schemes is an art. This manual focuses primarily on the science.

In this manual, I will describe how to build a strong, fully lugged chromoly steel bicycle. Lugs are pre-fabricated metal sleeves placed around the joints of the different bicycle tubes (Figure 1-1). Lugged frames are as strong as welded frames and are more forgiving from a technical standpoint to construct than non-lugged frames. However, lugs are only available in a few possible angles, so lugged bicycle construction is less versatile than non-lugged construction.

Figure 1-1: *The lugs that join together the front triangle of a bicycle frame. In this picture, there are two sets of lugs for two different bicycle frames. A complete bicycle frame built with these lugs is visible on the front cover of this manual.*

I will describe tube mitering and silver brazing. Mitering is a method of placing curved cuts at the ends of metal tubes so that they fit together with maximum overlap. Silver brazing (also known as silver soldering) is a simple way of bonding tubes together. Milling machines and expensive torches are not required for the methods presented in this manual. As a matter of fact, all the tools needed to build the bicycle frame presented in this manual cost less than $300. The steel tubing and other bicycle parts cost anywhere from $175 to $275 depending on the availability of retailers' specials.

I will provide the reader with a step-by-step walkthrough for the entire frame building process. Chapters 1 through 6 of this manual describe the theory behind frame building. Chapters 7 through 10 contain detailed directions.

I chose the frame presented in this manual for its ease of construction and inexpensiveness. For the most part, when ease of construction and inexpensiveness were at odds with each other, ease of construction won out. I present what I believe to be the easiest multi-geared bicycle frame to construct.

The frame I present in this manual will be lightweight (around 4 lbs [1.8 kg]) and have a classic geometry, meaning the top tube runs parallel to the ground. To minimize confusion, I made this manual as simple and concise as possible. I therefore do not present many frame-building configurations and options to the reader. I acknowledge that the frame presented here may not be the exact frame the reader wishes to build. My advice for the reader is to stick to the plan as closely as possible. The fewer deviations the reader makes from the plan, the better results he will obtain.

The frame presented in this manual can be built to just about any size the reader desires, but the geometry is ideally suited for a road bike, touring bike, commuter bike or cyclocross bike with 700c wheels ("road wheels"). Unfortunately, the bottom bracket height of the frame described in this manual is too low to accommodate the smaller 26-inch rims typical of a mountain bike. If 26-inch wheels are placed on this frame, the rider may nick a pedal against the ground when he rides around a corner. In addition, the distance between the chainstays is too narrow to accommodate the fatter tires typical of mountain bikes.

Mountain bike frames can be built by lugged construction. However, the mountain bike frame presents the frame builder with many more challenges than the typical road bicycle frame. Lugs specific for mountain bike geometry, which typically includes a high bottom bracket shell, sloping top tube, and long suspension forks, are much harder to find than lugs for road frame geometry. Also, to make the rear triangle of a mountain bike frame accommodate fat tires, the frame builder often has to bend lugs or tubing, which is not a beginner-level technique. If the first time frame builder wishes to ride his bicycle off road, I suggest he build a cyclocross frame using the techniques described in this manual. Once the reader has finished his first frame, he will have sufficient theoretical knowledge and the practice to experiment and build the frame with the features and geometry he wants.

In this manual, I do not describe the following: metal-inert-gas (MIG) welding, tungsten-inert-gas (TIG) welding, brass brazing, fillet-brazed (non-lugged) frames (though we will perform a few fillet brazes), slotted dropouts, construction of forks, aluminum framesets, titanium framesets, or carbon fiber framesets. To keep the cost of construction affordable, we will not use milling machines or expensive jigs. However, I will present the reader how to construct a simple, inexpensive jig for the rear triangle. We will not be using a fancy alignment table. Our standard for alignment will be simple and effective; if the front triangle lies in a single plane, the rear wheel is centered in the stays, and the rider can ride the bicycle without using his hands, then we have achieved adequate frame alignment.

One final note, if the reader is unfamiliar with the terminology in the preceding two paragraphs he should not worry or decide he lacks an adequate bicycle-related fund of knowledge required to build a bicycle frame. I will define most of these terms later on in the manual. This manual does assume (however) the reader is familiar with the following bicycle components: headsets, hubs, axles, rims, forks, cranks, pedals, seat posts, saddles, derailleurs, shifters, brake calipers, brake levers, stems, and handlebars. If any of these terms are unfamiliar to the reader, he should consult another reference to understand what these components do before proceeding with frame building.

Pronouns

In this manual, I refer to the builder and reader as "he." I do not intend to exclude or offend women readers or builders. "He" is a neuter pronoun, and in my opinion "he" reads better than "he or she."

Safety

Building a bicycle frame opens the door to a large set of potential hazards. Welders, braziers, and metal fabricators have much higher rates of occupational illness and injury than your typical overpaid office potato. Even small hand held power tools can devitalize human flesh rapidly. Some brazing rods contain cadmium which can caused kidney failure, bone loss, emphysema, lung cancer, and other serious illnesses. Heat applied to galvanized steel can release zinc oxide fumes that can cause metal fume fever. Brazing fluxes contain halogens and all sorts of nasty poisons that should not be eaten, inhaled, or absorbed though the skin. A poorly built frame can fail, causing the rider to wreck and sustain injury. Over the ages, workers using torches carelessly have caused thousands of deaths and billions of dollars worth of property damage through fires. The list of things that could go wrong goes on and on and on. Realistically, I cannot point out every possible hazard to the reader. Ultimately the frame builder is responsible for his own safety.

The best safety advice I can give the reader is: 1. Be careful and be mindful of your surroundings; 2. Learn about the properties of the products you are using. Obtain manufacturer's safety data sheets (MSDS) from the manufacturer if necessary; 3. Have a charged fire extinguisher on hand; 4. Read the manual and safety precautions for every piece of equipment you buy, borrow, or use; 5. Wear the correct personal protective equipment (PPE) recommended by MSDS and user manuals; 6. Do not attempt frame building while distracted, tired, or under the influence of drugs or alcohol; and 7. Perform all brazing, cutting, cleaning, and grinding in a well ventilated area.

If the frame builder follows these seven safety tips, he will reduce his chances of an accident but not completely eliminate all risk. Unfortunately, there are no guarantees in life. Even if the frame builder strictly follows all the directions in this book, he or she still risks physical or psychological injury or death from the frame building process or from subsequent frame failure. The author, editors, and any other entity associated with the printing, distribution or sale of this book do not accept any responsibility or liability for injury or death that may become the reader or frame builder.

Chapter 2: Bicycle Frame Anatomy and Physiology

Tube Nomenclature and Frame Angles

The Paterek Manual contains in-depth discussions of frame materials and bicycle frame design. This manual presents more of a "cook book" approach to frame building in which the overall frame design, but not the frame size, has been predetermined for the builder. Therefore, I will only cover the very basics here.

The tubes, angles, and other features of the bicycle frame are detailed in Figure 2-1. The figure contains abbreviations that are defined in the text below. We will use these abbreviations for the remainder of the manual.

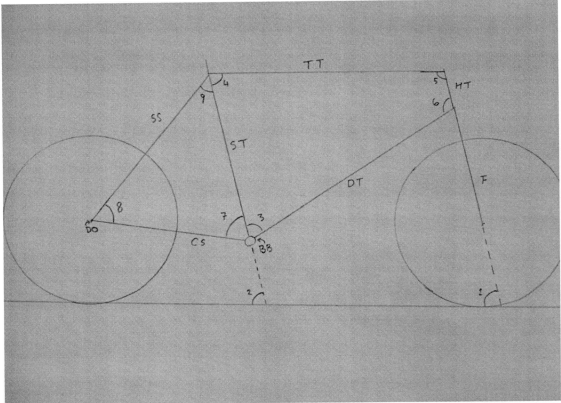

Figure 2-1. *Tubes and angle of a bicycle frame. Solid lines represent tubes. Letters refer to tubes or other frame parts. Dashed lines are imaginary lines, and numbers refer to angles.*

Metallic Parts

BB= Bottom bracket shell. The bottom bracket, pedals, and cranks all connect here. We will construct a bicycle with a lugged bottom bracket shell. The (vertical) distance between the BB and ground is known as the bottom bracket height. The (vertical) distance between the wheel axles and the BB shell is known as the bottom bracket drop.

ST= Seat tube. The seat post and saddle insert into the ST up top. The ST length is the main determinant of the height of the bike. Riders with short legs need frames with shorter ST. For the vast majority of lugged frames, the tube diameter of the ST must be as wide as (or wider than) the top tube (TT).

TT=Top tube. The TT can run parallel to the ground (classic geometry), or slant upwards. In this manual we will construct a frame with a classic geometry. The TT length is the main determinant of the length of the bike. Riders with long arms and long torsos need frames with longer TT.

DT= Down tube.

HT= Head tube (HT). The headset inserts here. The fork and front wheel are below, and the cockpit with handlebars and stem are above. For the vast majority of lugged frames, the tube diameter of the HT must be as wide as (or wider than) the DT and TT.

The ST, TT, DT, HT, and BB shell compose the front triangle of the bicycle. (Of course, the front triangle is a misnomer because the structure has four sides and not three). All intersections of the front triangle are joined by lugs.

F= Fork. Connects the wheel to the frame. We will not build a fork in this manual. We will assume that the builder has a fork with the exact length and rake to allow the TT to run parallel to the ground. In truth, this probably will not occur exactly. However, as long as the TT is more or less parallel to the ground, the resulting bicycle, when built-up with components, will have nearly the same size and handling characteristics predicted were our fork length prediction true.

SS= Seatstays. There are two, one on each side of the wheel. The SS are bridged with a brake bridge or stiffener.

CS=Chainstays. There are two. The CS are often bridged together with a chainstay stiffener.

DO=Dropouts. DO are placed at the intersection of the CS and SS. The rear wheel inserts here. For geared bikes, the openings in the dropouts are oriented vertically and have a derailleur hanger. Horizontal dropouts can allow for single speed applications without the use of an external chain-tensioning device. In this manual, we will construct a bicycle with lugged, vertical dropouts. For the purposes of this manual, we will use the term "slot" to refer to the opening in the dropout where the wheel axle is placed.

The DO, CS, SS, and BB shell compose the rear triangle. (Actually there are two rear triangles, one on either side of the rear wheel, but we refer to them as if there were only one).

Frame Angles

1= Head angle. The head angle is the angle of the HT relative to the ground. This angle is very important because it has a major influence on the handling characteristics of the bicycle. We will discuss the handling characteristics in more detail later on.

2= Seat angle. The seat angle is the angle of the ST relative to the ground. This angle does not influence the handling characteristics of the bicycle nearly as much as the head angle.

3= Seat tube-down tube (ST-DT) angle. This angle is fixed by the lugs of the bottom bracket shell, meaning once the frame builder has selected the bottom bracket shell he can no longer change this angle. (Actually, lugs can be bent a few degrees but I do not recommend the first time builder attempt this task).

4= Seat tube-top tube (ST-TT) angle. This angle is fixed by the ST-TT lug.

5= Top tube-head tube (TT-HT) angle. This angle is fixed by the TT-HT lug. Note that, in reality, this angle is obtuse meaning that the angle is greater than 90 degrees. However, we measure this angle as if it were acute (less than 90 degrees) by subtracting the true angle from 180 degrees. So a TT-HT angle measured with a protractor as 107 degrees is called a 73 degree TT-HT angle.

6= Down tube-head tube (DT-HT) angle. This angle is fixed by the DT-HT lug. The DT-HT angle, like the TT-HT angle, is obtuse but is named for its supplementary (180-the angle) acute angle.

7= Seat tube-chainstay (ST-CS) angle. This angle is fixed by the lugs of the bottom bracket shell.

8= Chainstay-seatstay (CS-SS) angle. In this manual we will build a frame with a lugged, articulated drop out which allows the builder full control of this angle without bending drops outs or stays.

9= Top tube-seatstay (TT-SS) angle. In traditional lugged frame construction, these are the only major joints of the frame that are fillet brazed and not lugged. These are also the last joints constructed, so this angle is really determined by all the other angles of the frame.

Not shown in figure 2-1 are the chainstay-chainstay (CS-CS) angle and the seatstay-seatstay (SS-SS) angle. The CS-CS angle is measured as half of the angle between the chainstays. For example, a frame with chainstays that form a 14 degree angle relative to one another and 83 degrees relative to the bottom bracket shell is said to have a 7 degree CS-CS angle. This is the one lugged joint that, for the purposes of this manual, we will not call "fixed." There is usually enough "slop" in the chainstay lugs of the bottom bracket shell to make small changes in the CS-CS angle to accommodate our desired chainstay length without actually bending the lugs. Longer chainstays require smaller CS-CS angles. The SS-SS angle, much like the TT-SS angle is determined by all other angles of the bicycle frame.

Frame angles remain the same regardless of the builder's approach or point of view. Hence, the ST-TT angle is the same angle as the TT-ST angle. In this manual, I will use different expressions of the same angle (such as ST-TT and TT-ST) interchangeably.

Common Lugged Bicycle Design Angles

The following are the most common lugged bicycle angle motifs:

Classic geometry: 73 degree head angle; 73 degree seat angle; top tube parallel to the ground; ST-DT of 60 degrees; DT-HT of 60 degrees; ST-TT of 73 degrees; TT-HT of 73 degrees.

Sloping top tube: top tube has a 6 degree slope relative to the ground; 73 degree head angle, 73 degree seat angle; ST-DT of 60 degrees; DT-HT of 60 degrees; ST-TT of 79 degrees; TT-HT of 79 degrees. This geometry is more common on mountain bikes because it allows for more stand-over clearance.

Lugs for the classic geometry are more common than for the sloping top tube. Road bikes usually have bottom bracket shells lugged for a ST-CS angle of 62 degrees. Mountain bikes, which require a higher bottom bracket, have bottom bracket shells lugged for a ST-CS angle of 67 degrees.

Lug Nomenclature

Throughout the remainder of this manual, we will use the following terminology when referring to lugs. The "ring" of the lug, occurs on the HT-DT and HT-ST lugs and is the location through which the frame builder places the head tube. A "socket" is any lug opening that accepts the end of a tube but is not a ring. Sockets usually have two concave and convex curves. A "point," as the name implies, is a convex curve of a socket that is in the shape of a point. "Deep" refers to a location on the inner surface of a lug. We often refer to the joint space between the tube and lug as being deep to the lug. A "window" is any hole in the lug that is not a socket or ring. Windows are useful because they let the frame builder physically see silver brazing alloy flow along a tube deep to the lug.

An Over Simplified Explanation of the Effects of Frame Design on Frame Intent and Frame Handling

For the intended purposes of this manual, an in-depth discussion of bicycle frame design is not necessary because the builder has no control over most of the angles of the bicycle frame because the angles are fixed by the lugs. However, the frame builder can affect some of the handling characteristics of the frame through the choice of chainstay and fork lengths.

The head angle helps determine the handling characteristics of the bicycle. A bicycle with a "steeper" or "tighter" head angle, closer to 90 degrees, has tight handling characteristics and can turn quickly. A bicycle with a "slack" head angle, closer to 45 degrees, will feel stable but turn slowly. Road bicycles and track bicycles are usually built to have tight handling characteristics and usually have head angles between 73 to 75 degrees. Downhill and freestyle mountain bicycles have slack head angles, around 69 degrees, so that they feel less twitchy while traveling at high speeds downhill. Cross-county mountain bicycles, touring bicycles, and cyclocross bikes have more intermediate handling characteristics and head angles, around 71 degrees.

The bottom bracket height is the distance between the bottom bracket shell and the ground beneath the rider. A bicycle with a low bottom bracket height is easer to mount and dismount. Commuter and cruiser bicycles have short bottom bracket heights for this reason. Mountain bicycles have high bottom bracket heights so that the rider is less likely to clip a pedal on rocks, roots, or uneven terrain. The bottom bracket height of the frame described in this manual assumes the builder will equip the bicycle with 700c (road) wheels. If he wishes to use 26 inch wheels, he will need to use short cranks to avoid nicking a pedal while taking corners, (or he can make adjustments using some of the measures discussed below).

A frame builder can raise the bottom bracket height by equipping the bicycle with a longer fork, but the head angle and handling characteristics will slacken a little. Likewise, he can lower the bottom bracket height by using a shorter fork, which would result in a steeper head angle and tighter handling characteristics. The frame builder can lower the bottom bracket height by using longer chainstays and raise it with shorter stays, but these changes have a much smaller effect per a unit of linear distance than the fork length.

Wheelbase is defined as the distance between the wheels where the tires touch the ground. Bicycles with shorter wheelbases handle tighter than bicycles with longer wheelbases. Because the length of the front triangle must be matched to the length of the rider's arms and torso, a frame builder who wishes to fine tune the wheelbase of a bicycle should do so through the length of the chainstays. Longer chainstays obviously create a longer wheelbase. The first time builder, however, should worry more about chainstay length as it relates to accommodating the correct tire width rather than perseverate on achieving some predetermined wheelbase to the nearest millimeter.

If the reader of this book wishes to make a cyclocross bike with fatter, off-road tires (35 to 45mm in width), he should use longer chainstays. Assuming the chainstays are straight and not curved, the distance between the two chainstays increases as we move away from the bottom bracket. Hence, shorter chainstays place the rear tire right next to the bottom bracket where the distance between the stays is at its minimum. Longer stays move the tire back a few centimeters, which creates more clearance for wider tires. Of course, if the frame builder elongates the chainstays, the bottom bracket will drop slightly, the wheelbase will lengthen, and the head angle and handling characteristics will slacken a little, which for a cyclocross bike, is not necessarily a bad thing.

Frame Materials

As a frame builder accumulates more experience, he develops very strong opinions and biases about frame materials. With this in mind, I will present the reader with the most objective description of bicycle frame materials possible.

Aluminum is the stuff that contains your cheap beer when you are not drinking it. Frames made of aluminum tend to create harsh rides with little vibration damping. The rider feels every nook and cranny in the road and, by the end of a long ride, feels pretty beat-up. Aluminum is a soft metal that is easy to machine. Aluminum's low melting temperature requires much less energy to weld than steel or titanium. These metallurgic characteristics allow industry to use aluminum to mass-produce cheap products yet market them as if they were state of the art. The weight savings of an aluminum frame are offset by harsh ride characteristics and a general lack of reparability.

Carbon fiber (graphite) is the stuff that comes in pencil leads. Carbon fiber is the frame material of choice for ill tempered roadies and gram counting weight weenies, (which are really one in the same). Carbon fiber can also be used to build seat posts, stems, wheels, crank sets, and even cycling shoes. A carbon framed bicycle with carbon components can cost about as much as a Toyota Corolla but is much less useful. This decade has seen the addition of carbon nano tubes into the resin of carbon fiber frames. Next decade, maybe we will see carbon pico tubes, and the decade after that, carbon famto tubes. Carbon fiber frame building kits do exist for the hobbyist and are comprised of straight tubes that fit in aluminum lugs with epoxy. In my extremely objective opinion, there are much cheaper ways to sniff glue.

Titanium is the stuff used to make grandma's artificial hip, spy planes, and nuclear submarines. Although titanium is strong, flexible, and resistant to corrosion, it is difficult to cut, impossible to torch braze, and tricky to TIG weld. Titanium is not the material of choice for the first time builder.

Steel is the stuff found in bridges, dams, and buildings. Steel can be cut, grinded, forged, cast, milled, welded, and brazed and is the material of choice for the infrastructure of civilization and the first time frame builder. Chromoly is a type of steel that contains chromium and manganese for increased strength and corrosion resistance. Although a bit heavy and susceptible to rust if neglected, chromoly steel bicycles are a joy to ride with the perfect amount of flexibility and excellent vibration damping characteristics.

Chromoly Tube Definitions and Parameters

Tube width is the outer diameter of the cross section of the tube in question. Wall thickness is the actual thickness of the metal wall of the tube. Tube width minus twice the wall thickness equals the inner diameter of the tube. The long axis of a tube is an imaginary line that passes along the entire length of the tube through the tube's center. The short axis of a tube is an imaginary line that passes through the cross section of the tube through the tube's center.

Some bicycle tubes are butted, meaning that the wall thickness and inner diameter varies down the length of the tube even though the tube width remains constant (figure 2-2). This allows for a lighter frame than regular straight gauge tubing, in which the wall thickness remains constant. Down tubes and top tubes are often double butted, meaning the wall thickness of the ends of the tube are thicker than the wall thickness in the middle. Seat tubes are often single butted, meaning that the wall thickness is thicker at one end of the tube than the other. The end with the thicker wall is inserted into the bottom bracket shell. Head tubes are generally thick, straight-gauge tubing. The thinner the wall thickness, the lighter the bicycle frame.

Figure 2-2: *A butted chromoly tube viewed from the end. The thickened butted wall creates the dark ring visible on the inside of the near end of the tube. The innermost area of the dark butt in this photo is the transition zone, where the wall thickness transitions from thick to thin.*

Tube widths for the front triangles of the more routine frame builds are as follows:

Standard road: 31.7mm (1.25") HT; 28.6mm (1.13") DT and ST; 25.4mm (1") TT.

Oversized road and lugged mountain bike: 31.7mm (1.25") HT and DT; 28.6mm (1.13") TT and ST.

Extra Large (XL): 31.7mm (1.25") ST and TT; 36mm (1.41") HT; and 35mm (1.38") DT.

In general, oversized and standard sized frames will only accommodate a fork with a steering tube of 25.4mm (1") diameter. The extra large frame accommodates a fork with the more common 28.6mm (1.13") diameter steering tube. There are a few lug sets out there that allow the builder to construct an oversized frame using a 36mm (1.38") HT for a fork with a 28.6mm (1.13") steering tube.

Small variations (0.1mm) in tube width are inconsequential for hand-built frames. For example, 31.7mm wide tubes and 31.8mm tubes are pretty much the same.

SS and CS are often tapered, meaning that tube width at one end is narrower than the other. The narrower ends connect to the dropouts. Some CS are oval, meaning that the cross section of the wider end is in the shape of an oval instead of a circle. The oval ends inserts into the bottom bracket shell. Others are "round-oval-round" meaning the drop out end and bottom bracket end are round, but the length that lies next to the tire is oval to allow more clearance. There are many other variations in the shape and sizes of CS including single bend, and S-bend, among others.

Chapter 3: Recommended Tools

To complete the bicycle described in this manual, the reader will need less than $300 worth of tools. Expensive milling machines and oxy-acetylene torches are not required. Tube-notching jigs and bi-metal-hole saws can be used to miter tubes, but their purchase price will push the total tool cost above $500.

The decision to buy high quality tools versus less durable, cheaper tools is an important dilemma for the first time builder. If the first time builder only wants to build a single frame, or is unsure if he will build more frames later on, the purchase of cheaper tools may be a sound financial option. If the first time builder knows he wants to make many frames, high quality tools are necessary because cheap tools wear out. Retailers such as Sears, Lowes, Home Depot, and Ace Hardware stock the whole spectrum of tools in terms of quality. Extremely affordable tools are available at Harbor Freight. The reader can also purchase used tools though newspaper ads or on-line classifies such as Craigslist or borrow tools from friends. Table 3-1 presents a list of tools required to build the bicycle frame in this manual. In addition to the tools in this list, the reader will need access to a Microsoft Widows® based computer and a printer.

Table 3-1: Recommended Tools

Tape measure (Figure 3-1)
Metric calipers (useful but not absolutely necessary)
Protractor (Figure 3-1)
Angle Finger (Figure 3-1)
Permanent magic marker
Scratch awl
Hammer
Drill (get one that uses a chuck, not the chuck-less variety)
Titanium nitride coated drill bits, at least three that are 1/8 inch thick or wider
Mineral spirits or other non-polar solvent
Small bench grinder (Figure 3-2)
Hacksaw (Figure 3-3)
Rotary tool with grinding bits and reinforced cutting wheel (Figure 3-3)
Half-round file (Figure 3-3)
One cylinder of methylacetylene-proadiene (MAPP) gas (Figure 3-4, Chapter 6)
MAPP-air torch with flexible hose (Figure 3-4, Chapter 6)
Spark lighter (Figure 3-4)
Five 1/16 inch x 18 inch 56% silver, cadmium-free brazing rods (Chapter 6)
        (These brazing rods can be found at a welding supply store such as Airgas)
Water soluble, silver brazing flux (Figure 3-4, Chapter 6)
Vice
A piece of angle aluminum
Epoxy
Two long straight pieces of angle steel, perforated with 3/8 inch (9.5mm) holes

Two C-clamps
One 3/8 inch (9.5mm) threaded rod
Two 3/8 inch x 2 inch (5.1cm) bolts
Sixteen 3/8 inch (9.5mm) nuts
Crescent wrench
Small vice grips
Small section of brake or shifter cable
One hose clamps
Thin rod of copper or steel, 12 to 16 inches in length
Toilet bowl cleaner that contains hydrochloric acid (do not drink)
Sandpaper and steel wool
Bucket
Many rags
Brushes with metal bristles
Rear brake the rider wishes to put on the frame
Rear wheel and tire the rider wishes to put on the frame
Cheap, rear wheel with the same axle length and rim size as the wheel above
Water bottle cage the rider wishes to put on the frame
Sturdy table (I use an old door nailed to a pair of saw horses)
All personal protective equipment recommended by user manuals and MSDS's

The aluminum angle protects the tubing from the jaws of the vice, (more on this later in Chapter 7). We use the angle steel, bolts, nuts, threaded rods, steel or copper rod, hose clamp, brake cable, and vice grips to construct improvised jigs. The builder should read Chapter 6 before purchasing a torch, flux, or brazing rods.

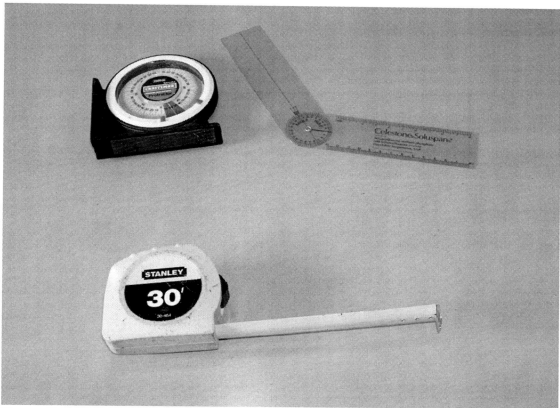

Figure 3-1: *Protractor, angle finder, and tape measure. We use the protractor to find the pitch angle of a tube relative to gravity (ground) and the angle finder to determine the angle of one tube relative to another.*

Figure 3-2: *A bench grinder is used for making rough miters. In truth you can get by without one by using a hacksaw and a half-round file instead, but the bench grinder will save you much time and effort. Small bench grinders are available new for around $35.*

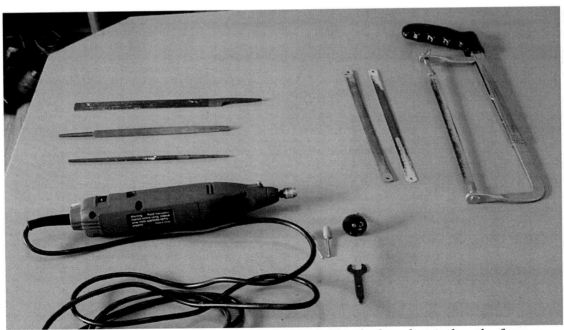

Figure 3-3: *Files, hacksaw, and rotary tool. Much like the bench grinder, the frame builder can use a hacksaw and files in place of a rotary tool at the expense of saved time and effort. A good rotary tool can be found new for less than $50. The frame*

builder will need a few reinforced cutting wheels and small and large grinding bits designed for metal. A regular drill equipped with a grinding bit is not an adequate substitute for a rotary tool.

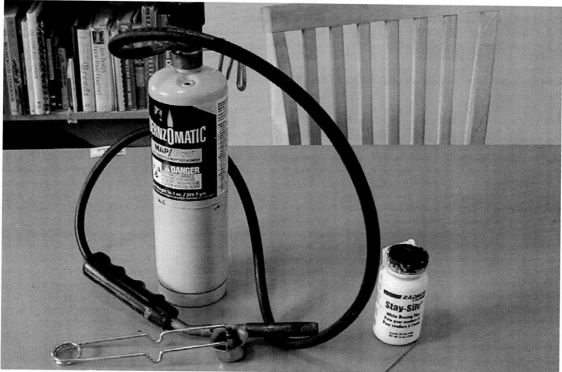

Figure 3-4: *A MAPP-air torch, spark lighter and silver brazing flux. Soldering flux is no substitute for silver brazing flux. The frame builder should find a torch with a flexible hose such as the one in the figure. Such a torch is more ergonomic than a torch that fastens directly on top of the MAPP canister without a hose. The frame builder can find a torch, MAPP gas canister, spark lighter combination pack for about $35.*

Chapter 4: Recommended Bicycle Tubing and Parts

The bicycle frame planned in this manual is a traditional standard-sized road frame with a classic geometry with shifter cables that run along the down tube. I chose this frame for its ease of construction and the high availability of the required tubing and parts. For the first time builder, I do not recommend any significant departures from the plans outlined below. I will present the first time builder with a few reasonable options that do not excessively complicate frame building or deviate greatly from the cookbook approach of this manual.

Bicycle tubes, lugs, bottom bracket shells, dropouts, and small braze-on parts are available online at Nova Cycles, Bikelugs.com, Henry James Bicycles, Ceeway Bike Building Supplies, and Bringheli Frames-Tools & Jigs (Chapter 12 contains detailed web addresses). Depending on the availability of web specials, all the necessary parts for a complete frame can be purchased from between $175 and $275.

Failure to follow recommended options decreases the first time builder's chance of success and may furthermore result in frame failure, injury, death, or a deep sense of shame.

Bottom Bracket Shell

I recommend the first time frame builder acquire a standard sized road lugged bottom bracket shell with the following features; lugs should fit 26.8 mm (1 1/8") DT and ST, and 22.2mm round (7/8") CS. The angles of the lugs should be: 60 degree DT-ST, 62 to 63 degree ST-CS, and 7 to 8 degree CS-CS (Figure 4-1). Acceptable alternatives to the preceding specifications include:

Option 1. The above sized lugs and angles with cable guides. This type of bottom bracket shell will save the frame builder some work.

Option 2. Above angles and lug sizes with 24mm oval chainstays, (which means the chainstays lugs are 30mm in height and 16mm in width).

Option 3. The above angles, with or without cable guides, round or oval chainstays, but with lugs to fit oversized tubes (31.8mm [1 ¼"] DT, 28.6mm [1 1/8] TT and ST).

Not recommended for the first time builder: stainless steel bottom bracket shells; lugless bottom bracket shells; or XL sized bottom bracket shells; mountain bike bottom bracket shells.

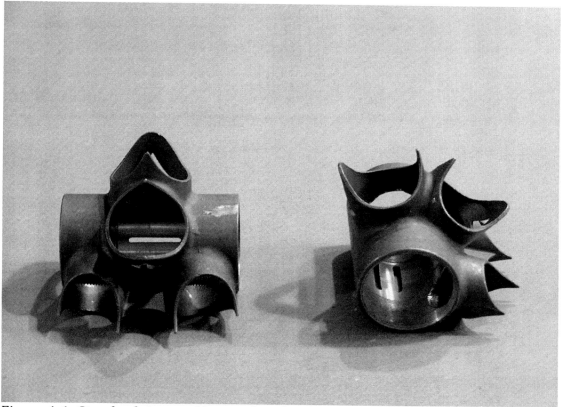

Figure 4-1: *Standard size road bottom bracket (two views). The first time frame builder should try to find one with cable guides if he can.*

Tubes of the Front Triangle

Obviously, tube size must correspond to the lugs of the bottom bracket shell. I recommend the first time builder find a tube set with tube widths of the standard size (31.7mm [1 ¼"] HT, 28.6mm [1 1/8"] DT and ST, and 25.4mm [1"] TT). The wall thickness of the head tube should be between 0.9 to 1.2mm, and the headset should be 200mm long. For the ST, DT, and TT, the wall thickness of the thick butted ends should be 0.8 or 0.9mm. The wall thickness between butts should be 0.5 or 0.6mm. The first time builder should try to find the longest tubes possible (up to 650mm) with the longest possible butts. Acceptable alternatives to the preceding specifications include:

Option 1. The above wall thickness but with oversized tubing (31.7mm [1 ¼"] HT and DT, 28.6mm [1 1/8"] TT and ST).

Option 2. The recommended wall thickness with oversized tubing but with a 36mm HT to accommodate a fork with a 1 1/8" steering tube.

Option 3. Standard sized or oversized tubing (with a 31.7mm HT), but rather than purchasing bicycle specific tubing, the frame builder can purchase straight gauge multi-purpose chromoly tubing from a metal supply shop. The wall thickness should be around 0.035 inches (0.8mm). The resulting frame will be cheaper to build but will weigh slightly more than a frame built with butted tubing.

Not recommended for the first time builder: XL sized tubing; very thin-walled (<0.5 mm) tubing; stainless tubing; heat treated tubing; externally butted tubing; tubing with very short butts; air hardened tubing; or any non-chromoly tubing.

Lugs of the Front Triangle

Obviously, the size of the lugs should correspond to the size of the tubes and the bottom bracket shell. I recommend the classic geometry with the following angles: 60 degree HT-DT; 73 degree HT-TT; and 73 degree ST-TT. Options for lugs of the front triangle include:

Option 1. Stamped lugs. While not as elegant as cast lugs, the first time frame builder will find that stamped lugs are easier to work with due to their loose tolerances and uniform wall thickness. Stamped lugs are usually half the price of cast lugs. By grinding the points off of stamped lugs, the frame builder can make them appear more elegant.

Option 2. Cast lugs with small windows (Figure 1-1, Chapter 1). The first time frame builder can use the small widows to ensure that the silver filler material properly penetrates the lug during brazing.

Option 3. Cast lugs without windows. Of the three options, the first time frame builder will find these lugs the most difficult to use.

Not recommended: stainless lugs; fancy artisan lugs with all sorts of curly cuts; or lugs with any angles different than outlined above.

Dropouts

For the first time builder, I recommend lugged, articulated, vertical dropouts (Figure 4-2). Horizontal dropouts make frame building easier because these drops allow the frame builder leeway in the position of the rear wheel axle, if the rear triangle is sub-optimally aligned. However, I do not know of any available lugged articulated horizontal dropouts on the market. Non-articulated lugged and plug-in style dropouts are plentiful but require the frame builder to bend the plug or lug of the seatstay to fine tune the CS-SS angle. Options for dropouts include:

Option 1. Lugged, articulated, vertical dropouts with lugs for 12.5mm CS and 10.5mm SS.

Option 2. Lugged, articulated, vertical dropouts with lugs for 12.5mm CS and 12.5mm SS.

Not recommended for the first time builder: dropouts requiring slotted stays; or stainless dropouts.

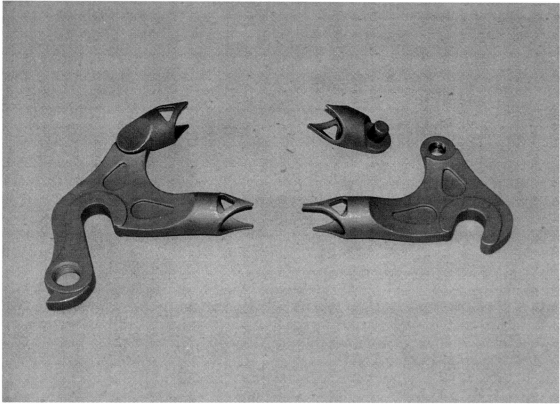

Figure 4-2: *Lugged articulated vertical dropouts. The articulated SS lug allows the frame builder to easily fine tune the CS-SS angle. However, the vertical dropouts allow one and only one location for the axle of the rear wheel. The frame builder must therefore be diligent and build a rear triangle with good alignment.*

Seatstays

Seatstays are generally tapered, with the smaller end plugging into the SS lug of the dropout. The size of the smaller end must correspond to the SS lug. For the first time builder I recommend straight, round seatstays. Options for seatstays include:

Option 1. Seatstays with tube widths of 10.5mm and 14mm for small and large ends, respectively.

Option 2. Seatstays with tube widths of 12.5mm and 16mm for small and large ends, respectively.

Not recommended: thin walled; curved; bent; non-round; stainless; or heat treated seatstays.

Chainstays

Much like seatstays, chainstays are tapered with the smaller end plugging into the CS lug of the dropout and the bigger end plugging into the CS lug of the BB shell. I recommend straight chainstays. The big end of the CS must correspond to the CS lug of the selected BB shell. Options for chainstays include:

Option 1. Completely round chainstays with small and big ends of 12.5mm and 22.2mm, respectively.

Option 2. Chainstays with small round ends of 12.5mm and big 24mm (30mm x 16mm) oval ends.

Not recommended: Round-oval-round chainstays; single bend or S-bend chainstays; heat-treated chainstays; or very thin-walled chainstays.

Additional Frame Parts

The frame builder will also need the following:
2 seatstay caps with plug-ins that correspond to the big ends of the seatstays
5 cable stops (Figure 4-3). The frame builder requires only three but they are easy to loose.
1 brake bridge for caliper brakes or 2 brake bosses for cantilever or V-brakes
2 water bottle bosses (optional, Figure 4-3).
2 gear lever bosses (Figure 4-3).

The frame builder can acquire two additional cable stops in place of gear lever bosses if he knows he will never use down tube shifters. However, gear lever bosses also work well to mount cable tension adjustors for STI shifters.

If the frame builder does not have cable guides on his BB shell he will need a small T-nut purchased at a hardware store. This T-nut is brazed onto the BB shell and fits into the hole of a plastic detachable cable guide purchased at a bike shop. Alternatively, steel cable guide kit can be brazed directly onto the BB shell.

Figure 4-3: *From left to right: cable guides (which are not really necessary), water bottle bosses (optional), gear lever bosses (may be substituted for cable stops), and cables stops (necessary for all bicycle frames except track bikes and fixies with no derallieurs or rear brakes).*

Chapter 5: Shaping Metal Tubes — Mitering and Drilling

Mitering Basics

In order to provide the strongest joint possible, the tubes and stays have to be cut in a special manner so that there is maximal overlap and minimal gaps between to two adjacent pieces. The method of cutting tubes for maximal overlap is called mitering. The frame builder should not attempt the miter described in this chapter until he has read and understands Chapter 7: Making the Front Triangle.

Imagine we want to join the head tube and down tube together at a 120-degree angle. Were we to simply place the down tube against the head tube at 120 degrees, they would intersect at a single point, which, if brazed, would make for a very weak joint. Making a single 60 degree cut at the end of the down tube would allow the two tubes to intersect at two points, which is still unacceptable. The frame builder must make a curved set of cuts in the end of the down tube, so that the two tubes intersect at a 120-degree angle without any gaps. This set of curved cuts is called a miter and the process of making these cuts is called mitering.

There are four general ways to miter a tube. The first method is to intuitively file or grind away at a tube until the pieces fit together. Using this method successfully is nearly impossible for the first time builder. The second is to purchase a milling machine. Inexpensive milling machines are available, but most do not accommodate the large-sized (28.6mm [1 1/8"] +) end mills required for frame building. Larger milling machines cost well over $1500. The third option is to use a combination tube-notching jig and bi-metal-hole-saw combination tool. Although cheaper than a milling machine, the required jig set-up, hole-saws, and ½" drill can cost over $300. I recommend this set up for the builder who successfully builds his first frame using this manual, enjoys the process, and knows he will build many more frames in the future. The fourth option is to use a combination of computer generated paper templates and simple hand and power tools to make the desired cuts. This method produces miters of the same quality as those made by tube-notching jigs but requires more time and effort. The computer-generated template method is effective and cheap and is the mitering method presented in this manual.

Mitering Using Computer-Generated Templates

Step 1: Obtain the computer program

The tube-mitering program we will use in this manual was written by the frame building, mathematical, and computer genius Giles Puckett. The program is called tubemitre.exe, and is open source and freeware. The program works on Microsoft Windows-based computers. Refer to the references section in the back of the manual for a web link to download tubemitre.exe or simply do a Google search for "tubemitre.exe." Be sure to read the supporting document.

<u>Step 2: Generate and transfer the paper template</u>

When the user first opens the application, a template corresponding to the program's default settings will appear. The user needs to change these settings. In the upper left hand corner of the tubemire.exe application window is a single pull down menu called "file." The first item under "file" is the "settings…" category. If the user selects this category, a smaller window will appear. In this window, the computer asks the user to input data. The first parameter is the diameter (tube width) of the tube that needs to be mitered. In this example, the tube being mitered will be the down tube. Assuming the frame builder is making a standard-sized bicycle frame, he will enter 28.6 mm. The second parameter is the wall thickness of the mitered tube. Because we are cutting into the thick-butted end, the frame builder should enter 0.8 or 0.9mm. The third parameter is the diameter (tube width) of the other connecting tube (in this case the head tube). The frame builder enters 31.7 or 31.8mm (assuming standard-sized tubing). The final parameter is the angle at which the tubes connect. If the frame builder wishes to place the center of the template on the top surface of the down tube, (which is what I recommend), he enters the true, obtuse DT-HT angle of 120 degrees. If he wishes to place the center of the template on the bottom of the down tube, he enters the "frame builder's conventional angle" of 60 degrees. Entering either 120 or 60 degrees will result in the same miter as long as the template is placed in the appropriate location.

Once the user enters the data, the computer will display an odd geometric shape with the settings written upon it. Under "file" the user can select "print" to print out the template. Because the computer presents the user with two possible curves, one "theoretical" and dashed, the other "real" and solid, the user must print using the highest quality print option for his printer. Otherwise both curves will appear solid and the user will not know which curve is which. The frame builder should locate the "real" curve, mark it somehow, and cut out the template (Figure 5-1).

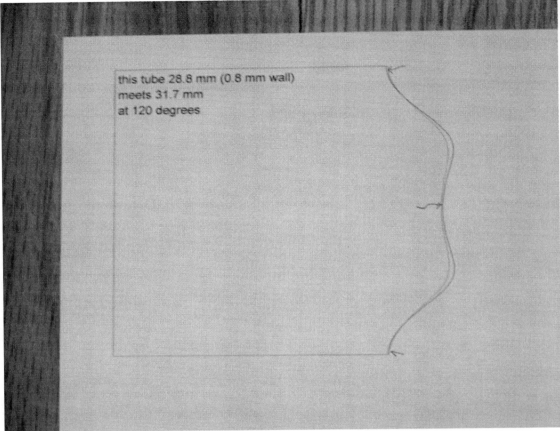

Figure 5-1: *A computer generated mitering template. The computer generates two curves. One represents a "theoretical" miter as if the tube has a wall thickness of zero. The other represents the "real" miter. Here, the frame builder marks the "real" curve with a pen (which is the curve on the inside at the middle of the template and on the outside at the far edges). The frame builder needs to cut out the entire template including the rectangular potion located opposite the miter curve.*

After the frame builder cuts out the paper template, he must place it on the down tube. He must ensure that the miter to be cut lies entirely on the thickened butt, looking inside the tube if necessary. If the template has been cut out properly, the corners of the straight, flat end of the template (opposite the curved potion) should meet up nicely. The template should be secured on the tube with tape (Figure 5-2).

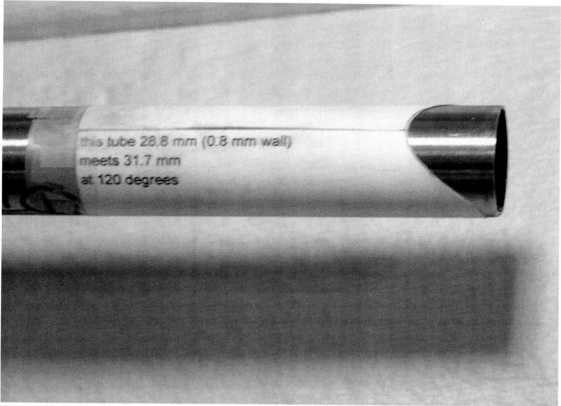

Figure 5-2: *The computer generated mitering template secured on the down tube with tape. In this photo, we are looking at what will be the bottom surface of the down tube. Note that the corners of the template on the side opposite the miter curve line up well.*

Step 3: The rough and fine miter

If the frame builder rotates the tube while examining the template, he will notice that the miter has two concave and two convex sections. The convex sections will lie along the sides of the head tube and are mirror images of one another. One of the concave sections is deeper compared to the concave section on the opposite side. The deeper concave section lies along the under surface of the down tube.

The frame builder should place the tube in a vice, so that one of the two concave sections of the template faces up. Using a hacksaw or rotary tool equipped with a cutting wheel, the frame builder should cut a V-shaped notch in the tube. This notch should not reach the edges of the template (Figures 5-3 and 5-4). When finished, the frame builder should rotate the tube and make a V-shaped notch on the other concave side.

Figure 5-3: *Cutting a V-shaped notch with a rotary tool. The frame builder should be careful not to cut into the template. Note that angle aluminum has been glued to the vice with epoxy to prevent the vice from scratching or denting the tube.*

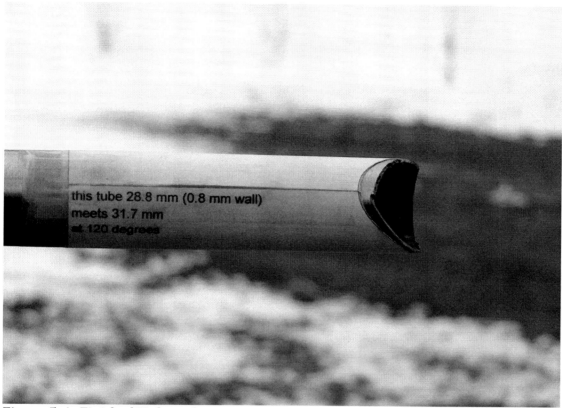

this tube 28.8 mm (0.8 mm wall)
meets 31.7 mm
at 120 degrees

Figure 5-4: *Finished V-shaped cut.*

After completing two V-shaped cuts, the frame builder should take the tube out of the vice and use the bench grinder to make a rough miter. The metal should be ground down to within 1 to 2mm of the edges of the template (Figures 5-5 and 5-6). When using a bench grinder, the builder should secure the tube on the built in rest. This step helps to eliminate unwanted chatter or movement of the tube and prevents the builder from grinding parts of the tube that are outside his field of vision.

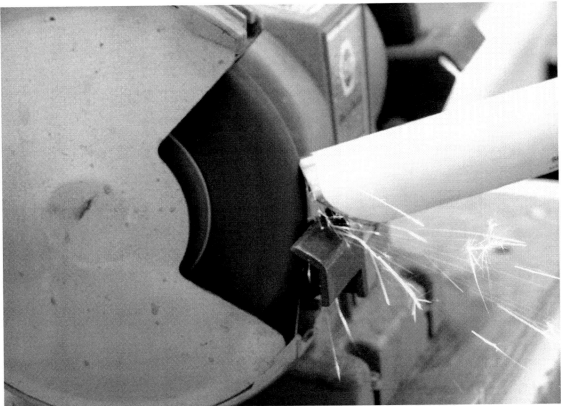

Figure 5-5: *The frame builder uses a bench grinder to grind in a rough miter. Eye protection is necessary during any type of grinding or cutting.*

this tube 28.8 mm (0.8 mm wall)
meets 31.7 mm
at 120 degrees

Figure 5-6: *Finished rough miter. The miter is close to, but not, touching the paper template.*

After completing the rough miter, the frame builder should place the tube in the vice so that the rough-mitered end faces upward. The frame builder should use a half-round file or rotary tool with a grinding bit to grind the edges of the miter down to the very edges of the template (Figure 5-7). If the frame builder is meticulous, he should be able to make an excellent miter, which when laid against the head tube, leaves small gaps no bigger than the thickness of a fingernail (Figure 5-8).

Figure 5-7: (*Top*) *The frame builder uses a rotary tool with a grinding bit to make a fine miter.* (*Bottom*) *Finished fine miter. The end of the tube has been ground down as close as reasonably possible to the edges of the template.*

Figure 5-8. *The head tube has been balanced on the mitered end of the down tube. Hardly any gaps are visible between the two tubes. Realistically, the frame builder should produce a miter that leaves no gaps wider than the thickness of a fingernail.*

Drilling Holes in Tubes

The first time frame builder has to learn how to drill holes in tubes to mount water bottle bosses and to make hot air vents and stress-relief holes. I wrote this manual assuming the first time frame builder does not have access to a drill press. Drilling holes in metal tubes with a hand drill can be tricky but, with practice, becomes routine.

Step 1: Marking and peening

In this example, I demonstrate how to make a hot gas vent on the head tube. This vent is useful when the frame builder brazes the top tube to the head tube and seat tube to complete the front triangle. Without this vent, the lugs cause the top tube to become a sealed cylinder. When the frame builder applies heat to the HT-TT joint, the air inside the top tube heats up and expands. Eventually, enough pressure builds up to push the top tube away from the seat tube or head tube, resulting in a front triangle with a different geometry than planned.

Once the frame builder determines where the top tube lies against the head tube, he makes the location of the vent on the head tube with a marker. Using his non-dominant hand, he holds the tip of a scratch awl over the mark. Using his dominant hand, he taps the end of the scratch awl with a hammer hard enough to leave a little dent or scratch (Figure 5-9).

Figure 5-9: *The frame builder peens the head tube to prepare for drilling a hot gas vent.*

Step 2: Drilling

The frame builder places the drill bit into the small dent. The small dent or scratch allows the titanium nitride coated drill bit to bite into the tube (Figure 5-10). Without the dent, the drill bit would roll off the tube when the drill is powered. When drilling, the frame builder must apply firm downward pressure but not so much pressure that the drill bit bows or breaks. After drilling a small hole, (1/8" is a good size to start), the frame builder can enlarge the hole with a thicker titanium nitride coated bit if desired. Generally, small holes are good enough to vent hot air, but larger holes are required to vent water that becomes trapped in the frame during cleaning.

Figure 5-10: *A peened scratch or dent allows the drill bit to bite into the head tube. Without the scratch or dent, the drill bit would roll off when power is applied.*

Chapter 6: Brazing Basics

Methods of Joining Metal Tubes

In general, there are three ways to join steel tubes: welding; soldering; and brazing. In welding, steel tubes are more or less melted together, and any filler material is the same or similar to the type of parent metal of the tubes. Most production bikes are welded using TIG (tungsten inert gas) welding machines. Although effective, TIG machines are usually too expensive for the frame building hobbyist. MIG (metal inert gas) welding machines are cheaper than TIG machines. Whereas TIG welders release heat and melt metal slowly, MIG welders release heat rather rapidly. This rapid release of heat can distort or burn holes in the thin walls of bicycle tubing. Unless the first time builder is an experienced MIG welder, he will be unable to successfully MIG weld a frame together.

In soldering and brazing, the steel tubes are not melted. Rather, they are joined together using a type of metal glue known as a filler alloy. The filler alloy is a metal that has a lower melting temperature than the steel tubes, so the frame builder can melt the filler metal into the gap between tubes without actually melting (or warping) the steel. The molten filler material fills the gap by capillary action.

In both soldering and brazing, heat performs two functions: First, it melts the filler material so that it can flow into the joint space. Second, the heat allows the parent metal of the tube to form a metallurgic bond with the filler metal. If the parent metal is not heated to the right temperature, molten filler metal will not form a strong bond.

Soldering and brazing require the use of a flux. Flux is a chemical mixture of reducing agents (usually fluorides) that reduces or sequesters oxides created by heat and combustion. Without flux, a soldered or brazed joint becomes contaminated with oxides and will be very weak.

Soldering uses a soft metal filler and, by definition, occurs at a temperature less than 450 C (800 F). Although soldered joints are too weak to join bicycle tubes, the frame builder can use soft solder for cosmetic purposes to fill small dents or create the illusion of seamless joints. However, if the frame builder wishes to powder coat his frame, he should not use soft solder because some solders melt during the powder coating process. Also, the frame builder should not perform any soldering until after finishing all the necessary brazing. Because steel is a good conductor of heat, brazing even at long distances away from soft solder can cause the solder to melt.

Brazing is essentially soldering at a higher temperature, greater than 450 C (800 F). The type of filler metals used in brazing is harder and tougher than soft solder. Unlike soldering, brazed joints are adequately strong for bicycle frame building.

Frame builders use brazing to form fillet joints and lugged joints. Fillet joints are constructed without a lug. The frame builder lays down a thick ring of filler material around the joint as reinforcement. A skilled frame builder can file down the fillet so that the frame appears seamless after painting. The vast majority of fillet joints use brass as a filler metal because molten brass forms fillets quite well.

However, oxy-acetylene torches are required to braze brass due to the metal's high melting temperature (850 C, [1600 F]). Oxy-acetylene torches cost at least $300, require special safety training (acetylene is inherently unstable), and are not recommended for the first time builder unless he enrolls in a supervised frame-building or torch-brazing class. Therefore, I do not cover brass brazing in this manual.

Silver brazing alloys contain silver in addition to copper, zinc, and other metals. Silver brazing is sometimes called "silver soldering." However, this name is technically incorrect because melting occurs over 450 C (800 F). A common frame-building misconception is that brass-brazed joints are always stronger than a similarly designed joint brazed with silver. This statement is only true when the frame builder selects the incorrect silver brazing alloy for the joint design or parent metal. For example, low silver containing alloys (5-25% silver) are designed to join copper and make very weak joints when used to connect steel or stainless steel. Compared to brass, which does not penetrate into small crevices very well, lugged joints are almost always stronger when the frame builder uses high-flowing, low-viscosity silver brazing alloy as filler. On the other hand, high flowing, low viscosity silver brazing alloy does not form large fillets well. However, good fillet-forming silver alloys (such as Fillet Pro SS®) are available and can form fillets that are even stronger than brass fillets. Silver fillets have even been used successfully for the structural components of racecar suspensions and airplanes. In this manual, we will construct a few fillet joints using high flowing, low viscosity silver alloy. Because these fillets are for smaller, low-stress joints, the use of silver alloy is acceptable.

Recommended Brazing Alloy

To successfully complete the bicycle frame described in this manual, the frame builder will require a silver-based brazing alloy with the following properties: 1. The melting temperature should be around 1200F to permit the use of an inexpensive MAPP-air torch; 2. The alloy should be designed for torch brazing and not vacuum-furnace brazing; 3. The alloy should have a high content of silver (45%+); 4. In molten form, the alloy must be able to flow into small spaces by capillary action; and 5. For safety purposes, the alloy should be cadmium free.

Safety-Silv 56® by Harris® is a brazing rod that contains 56% silver and meets all the above criteria. This brazing rod is sold at welding supply stores such as Air Gas and comes in 1/16" thick rods or coils. A length of 67" corresponds to about 1 troy ounce (31g). A pack of five 1/16" thick, 18" long rods (a total of 90", 1.34 troy oz) costs about $35 but is more than enough filler material to complete a lugged bicycle frame in the hands of a practiced brazier. The nickel-silver brazing rods found at most hardware stores have high melting temperatures, contain very little silver, and are not adequate substitutes for high silver-content brazing alloy.

Recommended Brazing Flux

I recommend brazing flux with the following characteristics: 1. The flux should be water soluble for ease of cleanup; 2. The flux should be formulated specifically for silver brazing and be active at 1200F; and 3. The flux should come as a paste for ease of application.

Two products by Harris®, Stay-Silv White® flux and Stay-Silv Black® flux, meet these requirements. Stay-Silv White®, as the name implies, is white in color and is the flux that appears in the photographs of this manual. Stay-Silv Black® is actually dark brown in color and is a little more expensive than Stay-Silv White®. Of the these two fluxes, Stay-Silv Black® is probably more forgiving for the first time builder who will likely use too much heat during brazing and risks exhausting his flux. Soldering flux purchased at a local hardware store is water soluble but is not active at the correct temperature. I do not recommend the first time frame builder use flux-coated brazing rods in place of a jar of flux paste.

Recommended Torch and Fuel

I recommend methylacetylene-propadiene (MAPP) gas as a fuel source for the first time frame builder. When burnt in air, MAPP gas produces a flame of 3600F (2000C), which is more than adequate for silver brazing. This flame is not hot enough for brass brazing, however, which requires an oxy-acetylene flame with a temperature of 5600F (3100C). MAPP gas cylinders are cheap ($8 to $10), universally yellow in color, and found in most hardware stores. MAPP gas is much more stable than acetylene and safer to use, store, and transport. Also, compared to the hotter oxy-acetylene flame, a MAPP-air flame is less likely to overheat a subassembly brazed by an inexperienced frame builder. Overheating can distort metal and exhaust flux. MAPP-air torches produce a broad flame desired for heating the large surface area of lugs. For easy ergonomic use, I recommend a MAPP torch with a flexible hose such as the Bernzomatic MAPP Torch Hose Pressure Regulated Torch Unit® (Figure 3-4). The frame builder can hook the canister on his belt and effortlessly move the torch with his hand.

Silver-Brazing Technique

In brazing, the proper sequence of events is: 1. Design the joint; 2. Build the joint; 3. Clean the joint; 4. Flux and assemble the joint; 5. Heat and braze the joint; 6. Slowly cool the joint; and 7. Remove flux and clean the assembly.

Practice is the key to developing good brazing technique. Fortunately, brazing low temperature high flowing silver alloy is probably the easiest metal joining skill to acquire, even easier than soft soldering. The key for the inexperienced brazier, is not to waste expensive silver brazing alloy. The following tips will guide the novice brazier to place his silver in the correct location.

<u>Tip 1: Design and prepare the joint within the correct tolerances</u>

For any given type of assembly brazed with high-flowing silver brazing alloy, the strongest joint occurs when a gap of 0.003 inches (0.08mm) occurs between the connecting parts. Smaller gaps will not allow complete penetration of filler metal and result in voids. In larger gaps, the strength of the joint is determined largely by the (weaker) tensile strength of the brazing alloy rather than the (stronger) metallurgic bond between parent metal and filler alloy. High flow brazing alloy will not fill very large gaps, which require a fillet.

Measuring the gap everywhere between a lug and a tube is impractical, if not impossible. However, a lugged joint is such a robust design, with large surface area overlap, and silver brazing alloys are so strong, (the weak stuff has a tensile strength of 30,000 psi), that gaps larger than 0.003 inches (0.08mm) still allow a very strong joint as long as the gap is not so large that the silver cannot fill it. When grinding out the inside of lugs, a good rule of thumb is to remove enough metal so that the frame builder does not have to strain himself to insert the tube into the lug. On the other hand, the frame builder should not remove so much metal that the tube rotates within the lug with almost no effort at all.

<u>Tip 2: Thoroughly clean the joint before assembling</u>

Paint, metal shards and filings, oil, grime and other debris will burn and create oxides in the presence of heat. Brazing flux has a cleaning effect on the joint by sequestering oxides that can contaminate the joint and create a weak braze. However, even a generous application of flux quickly becomes exhausted if the joint is not cleaned prior to brazing.

Manufacturers often oil metal tubing to prevent rust and corrosion. Prior to brazing, the frame builder should remove all traces of oil by rubbing the tube down with a clean rag soaked in mineral spirits. The frame builder should file off burrs and metal shards, which have high surface area and oxidize quickly, from the machined edges of tubes and lugs. Loose debris can be simply wiped or brushed off.

Paint, rust, or scale can be removed with an abrasive such as steel wool, sandpaper, or a metal brush.

The frame builder can use any brand of toilet bowl cleaner that contains hydrochloric acid to remove thick scale, oxides, or other dirt not easily removed by an abrasive. I recommend the frame builder pour a small amount of toilet bowl cleaner onto the steel and spread the liquid around with a metal brush until it completely covers the area in question. The builder should allow the toilet bowl cleaner to sit for two minutes before briskly scrubbing with a brush. If necessary, the frame builder can repeat this sequence a second or third time until the metal surface is bright and shiny. This method will clean, in minutes, stains that cannot be sanded off in hours. All acid residues and the inert ingredients of toilet bowl cleaner should be completely rinsed off with water. Acid residues left on tubing can combine with flux and other chemicals and detergents to produce toxic vapors. Some frame builders go as far as to neutralize acid residue with ammonia-based window cleaner or baking soda solution. However, when acids react with bases (alkali), the result is an inorganic salt that can cause corrosion.

Tip 3: Apply a liberal amount of flux

Flux is the frame builder's loyal friend. The frame builder can never use too much flux. Compared to silver brazing alloy, flux is very cheap. Not using enough flux, causes the flux to become quickly exhausted (completely saturated with oxides) during brazing. Silver, or any other filler alloy for that matter, will not bond to steel through exhausted flux (Figure 6-1). When flux becomes exhausted, the frame builder may have to cool, clean, re-flux, and re-braze the subassembly, wasting much time and effort. In severe cases, the frame builder may even have to un-braze the subassembly and clean exhausted flux from the inside of the lug. This process is a huge hassle and is best avoided.

Figure 6-1: *Exhausted flux during the brazing of a head tube (top horizontal), down tube (diagonal) subassembly. The dark discoloration where the down tube inserts into the lug is where the frame builder either applied too much heat or not enough flux, causing the flux to become completely saturated with oxides. The small lump at the edge of the lug is silver brazing alloy that could not bond to steel through the exhausted flux.*

As a general rule, the frame builder should flux the end of the tube (Figure 6-2, top) and the inside of the lug before assembly. After assembly, the frame builder should flux the outside of the lug and any steel within three to four inches of where heat will be applied (Figure 6-2, bottom). Oxides that adhere to un-fluxed steel are very difficult to remove compared to oxides sequestered in flux.

Figure 6-2 *Top: The frame builder applies a liberal amount of flux to the mitered end of the tube (seat tube), and the inside of the lug (not shown) prior to assembly. Bottom: After assembly, the frame builder applies flux to all steel surfaces within three to four inches of the joint.*

Tip 4: Apply the correct amount of heat

Unlike the oxy-acetylene torch that can produce flames that vary in temperature and composition (such as the neutral, carburizing, and oxidizing flames), a MAPP-air torch only produces one type of flame,. Although the temperature of the MAPP-air torch cannot be changed, the frame builder can change the overall heat output by opening and closing the valve regulator. A small flame, (the regulator barely open), is short and quiet, and puts out a small amount of heat. With the regulator fully open, the MAPP-air torch puts out a long, noisy, roaring flame, and has a high heat output. The color of the flame is always light blue and does not change much based on flame size. When brazing outdoors during a sunny day the frame builder might not even be able to see the flame and may have to judge flame size based on sound alone.

Too small a flame, with low heat output, will cause the steel subassembly to heat up very slowly. If the heat output of the torch is low during the brazing of a lugged joint, the frame builder risks heating only the edges of the lug, and the silver may not penetrate the full length of the lug. The result is a weak joint that may fail.

Too large a flame, with too much heat output, can have two negative consequences: First, the flux may become exhausted before the frame builder has finished brazing the subassembly. Therefore, oxides can build up preventing the silver from penetrating the joint. Second, the frame builder may heat to brazing temperature steel located in the wrong location. When the frame builder applies the silver brazing rod, the silver will melt and flow into all areas of high heat, including the desired joint and other hot areas where the alloy is not needed (Figures 6-3 and 6-4). Silver outside a joint does not weaken the frame but requires additional time for clean up. Silver brazing alloy is also very expensive and easily wasted in this manner.

Figure 6-3: *A down tube, head tube subassembly after brazing and cleaning. This subassembly was well brazed. Note that the silver, (which appears lighter than steel), does not extend long distances away from the immediate edges of the lug. The small globs of silver at the point of the lug can be filed off.*

The appearance and color of the flux and steel provide the frame builder important clues about the temperature of the subassembly. For Stay-Silv White®, cool flux is white and pasty (Figure 6-2). As the frame builder applies heat to the subassembly, the outer surface of the flux becomes confluent and smooth and changes color from white to clear (Figure 6-4). Once clear, the flux can never turn white again, even after cooling. The clear flux is active and sequesters oxides generated by the heating process. When the flux is clear, the sub-assembly is either right below or right at silver brazing temperature. A master brazier will keep the flux this color for the entire brazing process. A novice, however, will likely have to apply a little more heat to ensure that the silver penetrates fully into the lugged subassembly. As the flux become hotter, it sequesters more oxides and starts to turn yellow-green. At this appearance, the silver brazing alloy should readily melt and bond to the subassembly. Unfortunately, the green appearance also means that the brazing-flux is approaching exhaustion. Beyond green, the flux turns brown and then finally takes on a black, burnt appearance (Figures 6-4 and 6-1). The black, burnt-looking flux is completely exhausted. Of coarse, silver alloy cannot pass or bond through exhausted flux (Figure 6-1). If the exhausted flux occurs in the joint space, (deep to the lug, between the lug and tube), or where the brazing rod must be introduced in order to fill to the joint space, (usually at the edge of a lug), the brazing attempt has failed. The brazier will need to clean, reflux and re-braze the subassembly. Exhausted flux elsewhere, (outside the joint space or away from lug edges), will not impede the flow of brazing alloy but may indicate that the flux in the joint space is at risk of exhaustion.

Figure 6-4: *A seat tube (bottom), top tube (top) subassembly that was slightly overheated. The flux has turned black in places. The lightly colored, slightly lumpy metal immediately underneath the lug is silver brazing alloy. The clear globular substance underneath the silver is active flux. The white, bubbly, granular substance at the far bottom and left of the subassembly is brazing flux that never reached brazing temperature. Overall, this subassembly is acceptably brazed with good penetration, but the frame builder wasted a little of his expensive silver-brazing alloy.*

A brazier can salvage green or brown flux by cooling the subassembly, applying more flux, and resuming the brazing process. Upon reheating, brown flux will become green and green flux will become clear. Exhausted flux is seldom salvageable in this manner however.

Stay-Silv Black® flux remains active at higher temperatures than Stay-Silv White®. Black resists overheating longer than White and is probably easier to use for the first time builder. Other than the fact that Black is dark brown when first applied, color transitions are the same as for White, (clear, yellow-green, brown, crusty burnt black).

In outdoor light, steel at silver-brazing temperature may have a subtle yellow tint. (I've never actually seen this tint myself, though). In very low light conditions, steel at this temperature will have a very faint red glow. In outdoor light conditions, dull red steel is slightly overheated. The frame builder can certainly silver braze steel at this color, but he will have less control over the flow of silver and risks exhausting flux rapidly. Bright red steel is way too hot for silver brazing (but perfect for brass brazing).

Tip 5: Never put the silver-brazing rod in the flame

Proper brass-brazing technique often requires the frame builder to place the brazing rod between the torch flame and the subassembly. This method should never be used during silver brazing. Compared to typical brass brazing rods, silver brazing rods have a much smaller mass per unit length and much lower melting temperature. A silver-brazing rod placed in between a flame and subassembly will heat to melting temperature long before the steel is hot enough to permit bonding. The silver will not stick to the metal and will likely drop off the subassembly, resulting in nothing more than an expensive mess.

Tip 6: Make the silver dance

The three factors that determine the flow direction of molten silver alloy are heat, gravity, and the availability of active flux. Flux, unlike silver, does not defy gravity. A brazier should place extra flux, a reservoir of sorts, uphill from the joint. This extra flux can flow into the joint as the flux within the joint reaches exhaustion.

Heat is a stronger directional determinant than gravity during the brazing of high flow silver alloy. A brazier can easily draw silver upward against gravity by way of capillary action by placing the flame at a location uphill from the brazing rod. However, gravitational forces become stronger than cohesive forces when the brazier creates a large pool or puddle of molten silver. Some of the silver of a large pool can be pulled uphill, but the majority has a tendency to drip off the subassembly, an expensive waste. A good brazier can prevent the formation of a large pool by placing the brazing rod at the very edge of the lug, (where the lug meets the tube), while placing the flame on the body of the lug (Figure 6-5). Assuming the space deep to the lug has reached brazing temperature, and the tube away from the lug is cooler, capillary action will draw molten silver into the space deep to the lug (without the formation of a puddle on the outer surface of the tube).

Figure 6-5: *Proper placement of the torch flame and brazing rod during the brazing of a chainstay, dropout subassembly. This photograph was taken outdoors in daylight, so the flame is barely visible. Note that the brazier is pointing the torch at the body of the lugged dropout and is not placing the brazing rod directly in the flame. The brazing rod is placed at the edge of the lug. When dropout reaches brazing temperature, the silver will melt and flow uphill against gravity into the space between the chainstay and dropout lug, deep to the lug.*

A brazier can see silver melt and bond to metal at the edge of a lug, but he cannot see filler alloy move deep to the lug. The proper movement of the torch and heat is the key to good penetration of silver into the lugged joint space. When the frame builder begins brazing a cold subassembly covered with fresh white pasty flux, he should move the torch flame around the body of the lug in a systematic manner, heating the entire lug as evenly as he can. He should get the flux on the entire outer surface of the lug to turn clear as evenly as possible. At this point, the entire lug will be near brazing temperature. The frame builder should place the brazing rod at one edge of the lug, and move the flame along the body of the lug to draw the silver deep to and through the lug. If heated properly, he should be able to see the filler material emerge from the edge at the other end of the lug. The frame builder can then repeat this process on the topside, opposite side, and bottom side of the lug. A good silver brazier can draw silver throughout the entire lug by the movement of heat alone, introducing silver alloy into the lug at a single point and watching filler emerge from all other edges. When the frame builder is confident that he has achieved good penetration of filler alloy throughout the entire lugged joint space, he should allow the subassembly to cool slightly, just below brazing temperature, and inspect it. If necessary, he can reheat and re-braze any lug edges with small gaps. The frame builder should be careful, however, not to draw out silver from the space deep to the lug.

Removing Flux from a Brazed Subassembly

After brazing, flux contains reactive reducing chemicals and sequestered oxides that can corrode a subassembly. The frame builder must remove these chemicals as soon as possible. First, the subassembly needs to cool slowly to room temperature. Quenching a hot subassembly in water causes the steel to become hard and brittle. When cool, the frame builder can soak the subassembly in a bucket of water. Warm water removes water-soluble flux faster than cold water. Large globs of flux can be scraped off with a metal brush. Although the subassembly can literally rust before the frame builder's eyes during this process, this rust is superficial and easily removed with an abrasive. Exhausted flux, oxides that adhered to un-fluxed steel, and rust in hard to reach places is best removed with toilet bowl cleaner (Tip 2 above).

Chapter 7: Assembling the Front Triangle

At this point of the manual, I assume the frame builder is familiar with Chapters 5 and 6, understands mitering and brazing, and has acquired all the required tools, brazing rods, flux, lugs, tubes, and other frame parts.

Work Table Set Up

All grinding and brazing should occur in a well-ventilated area, outdoors if necessary. The vice and bunch grinder must be securely bolted to a sturdy worktable.

The frame builder must prepare the vice so that the hard steel jaws do not crimp, scratch, or dent the lugs or tubes. With a hacksaw, the frame builder should cut off two strips from the angle aluminum. Each strip should be slightly longer than the width of the vice jaws. The cut ends of the strips should be filed smooth. The frame builder should mix his epoxy, and apply a thin layer to the vice jaws and the inside of the angle aluminum. A cross section of typical angle aluminum is usually in the shape of an "L" with one long lip and a short one. One strip of angle aluminum is placed on each vice jaw so that the long lip covers the gripping surface and the short lip covers the top. The jaws should be closed slowly, ensuring the aluminum does not slip. The frame builder should torque down the handle so that the aluminum strips are clamped against each other tightly. The frame builder should allow 15 hours to let the epoxy cure. Viewed from above, the end product should look similar to the vice in Figure 5-9 and Figure 7-3.

The frame builder should keep his tools well organized. I keep my tools in three different boxes: One for brazing supplies, one for clamps and measuring devices, and the last for tools that help shape metal (files, scratch awl, hammer, etc). When finished using a tool, the frame builder should return it to the appropriate box. A cluttered workspace leads to misplaced tools, frustration, and wasted time.

Identifying and Marking Tubes

The frame builder needs to identify the tubes of his frameset and mark guidelines. The head tube is the shortest tube. For a standard sized tube set, there will be two "fat" tubes and one "skinny" tube. The "skinny" tube is the top tube. For an oversized tube set, there are two "skinny" tubes and a "fat" tube. The "fat" tube is the down tube. For both standard and oversized tube sets, the down tube is usually the longest tube. If the tube set is butted, the seat tube is the only tube with wall thicknesses that are different at each end. The frame builder should mark the seat tube "ST" and write "top" near the end with the thinner wall thickness. The down tube and top tube should be marked "DT" and "TT" respectively.

The frame builder needs to identify the long and short butts of the TT and DT. Some tube manufacturers mark the short butt with paint. The frame builder should peer inside the tube, identify the transition zone of the butt (Figure 2-2), measure the length of the butt by placing the end of a tape measure inside the tube, and mark the location of the transition zone of the butt on the outside of the tube. This procedure is especially important for the construction of smaller frames where the frame builder risks cutting a tube off beyond the butt. Of course, the top of the seat tube will not have a butt or a transition zone.

Guidelines down the long axis of the top tube and down tube are very useful. A similar guideline is not really needed for the seat tube. The frame builder should place the DT and TT side by side on a flat level surface with either end of the (usually) shorter top tube flush against the short butt of the down tube. Using his non-dominant hand, the frame builder should pinch the tubes in the middle so that they rest securely against one another. Using his dominant hand, he should place the tip of a permanent magic marker at the intersection of the two tubes and use the tube intersection as a straightedge to draw a straight guideline down the long axes, making sure the felt tip leaves marks on both tubes (Figures 7-1, 7-2). Being careful not to allow the tubes to roll against one another, the frame builder repeats the process at the other end. The frame builder does not need to extend the guideline all the way down to the end of the long butt of the down tube.

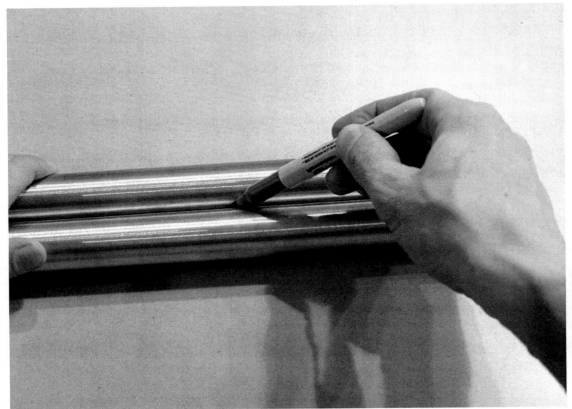

Figure 7-1: *Drawing the guidelines down the long axis of the top tube and down tube. The tip of the marker must leave marks on both tubes. When the frame builder moves*

the marker to mark the opposite end of the tubes, he must be careful not to let the tubes roll against one another.

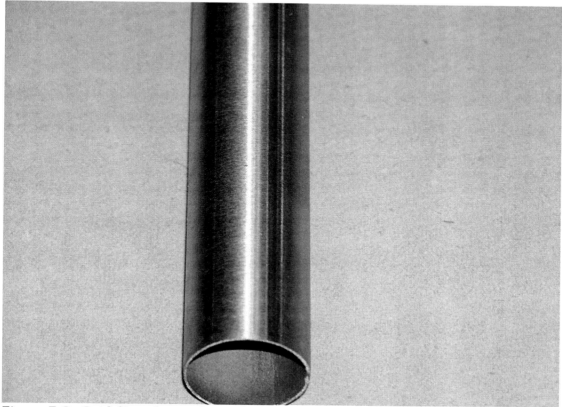

Figure 7-2. *Guidelines drawn down the long axis of the top tube and down tube are very useful. This guideline was constructed using the method shown in Figure 7-1.*

Identifying the Lugs

The frame builder needs to correctly identify his lugs or his frame-building attempt will end in disaster. The vast majority of ST-TT lugs double as ST collars and have "eyes" to accommodate a constrictor bolt (Figure 1-1, left). For classic geometry, the TT-HT lug (Figure 1-1, right) angle is closer to a right angle (90 degrees) than the DT-HT lug (Figure 1-1, center).

Determining the Size of the Front Triangle

For the purposes of this manual, tube lengths of a constructed frame are measured center-to-center (c-c), meaning that a tube is measured from the center of the intersections of the adjacent tubes. For example, a seat tube is measured from the center of the bottom bracket shell, where the bottom bracket spindle would lie, to the middle of the intersection of the top tube.

Custom fitting a frame to the anatomy of a rider can be an extremely complex task. Books have been written on the subject, and people spend hours in certification classes to master this skill. The first time builder should focus on getting the front triangle dimensions within the "ballpark" of the best fit for the rider's anatomy. The rider can fine tune the fit by seat post and stem selection. The resulting bicycle should fit the rider better than a stock-sized bicycle.

The length of the rider's legs and desired stand over clearance determine the seat tube length. Torso length, arm length, and riding position (streamlined versus upright) determine top tube length. For a frame with classic geometry, down tube and head tube lengths are determined by the size of the seat tube and top tube.

In Table 7-1 below, I provide the first time builder with estimates of front triangle tube lengths for a road frame based on rider height and inseam. These are ballpark figures and are not meant to be exact. These figures also assume the rider's torso, arms, and legs are well proportioned.

Rider Ht.	Inseam	ST	TT	DT	HT
5'2"	28"	48	48	53	7.5
5'4"	29"	50	50	55	8.0
5'6"	31"	53	53	58.5	8.25
5'8"	32"	56	56	62	8.5
5'10"	33"	58	58	64	9.0
6'0"	34"	60	60	66.5	9.25
6'2"	35"	62	62	68.5	9.5

Table 7-1: *Dimensions (length, measured c-c in cm) of the tubes of the front triangle by the rider's height and inseam. In this table, inseam is the actual measurement of the rider's anatomy and not his pant size. The frame builder should not despair if the down tube measurement on this table is longer than his purchased tube. Center-to-center measurements include parts of adjacent tubes.*

Another option to determine front triangle size is to model frame size based on a frame that already fits the rider well. The frame builder can adjust the seat tube and top tube length per the rider's request. The frame builder should keep in mind, however, that the model frame might not have a classic geometry.

If a frame builder remembers his high school trigonometry, he can use a spreadsheet to calculate more exact c-c tube lengths, dissecting the front triangle into right angle triangles. Once the frame builder formulates a working template, he can use the same spreadsheet over and over again, changing the numbers for each frame build.

The Head Tube-Down Tube Subassembly

When building the down tube-head tube subassembly, the guideline drawn along the long axis of the down tube should face upward, toward the top of the frame. The frame builder needs to use the software tubemiter.exe to create a template for the down tube miter (Chapter 5). I recommend entering an angle of 120 degrees to allow placement of the middle of the template along the top surface of the down tube. The other parameters entered into tubemiter.exe depend on the tube size, (standard versus oversized). In addition to locating and labeling the correct miter curve (real versus theoretical), the frame builder should place a mark in the middle of the template, at the center of the miter concavity (Figure 5-1). The frame builder should align this mark with the guideline at the short butt end of the down tube and secure the template in place with tape (Figure 5-2). If the down tube is going to be very long, for a tall rider, the template should be placed as close as possible to the end of the tube. If the down tube must be very short, for a short rider, the template must be placed as close as possible to the transition zone of the butt. The frame builder, however, should be careful to place the entire miter curve on the thickened butted end of the down tube.

If necessary, the frame builder can cut off any steel beyond the template with a hacksaw. The frame builder should follow the directions in chapter 5 to finish this miter (Figures 5-3 to 5-6). When finished, the head tube should balance on the down tube with minimal gapping (Figure 5-8).

The frame builder should attempt to assemble the head tube-down tube subassembly. More often than not, the HT-DT lug will be too tight to allow insertion of the head tube or down tube. If this occurs, the frame builder should place the lug in the vice and grind out the inside of the lug with a rotary tool or half round file until the tubes fit (Figure 7-3). Chapter 6, Tip 1 about good joint tolerances describes criteria for good fit. Grinding will create a rough surface on the inside of the lug. This rough surface will actually increase the surface area and strength of the joint, provided the joint is clean (Figure 7-4). If the frame builder accidently grinds out too much metal so that the head tube and down tube loosely insert into the lug with slop, the frame builder can tighten the fit by bending the point of the lug slightly to secure the down tube or by deforming the ring of the lug to secure the head tube.

Figure 7-3: *Removing metal from the inside of the lug that is too tight to allow insertion of the tubes. The frame builder should be careful not to leave unsightly tool marks on the outside of the lug. This task can be performed with a rotary tool or a half round file.*

The edges of the miter should line up well with the inside contours of the lug when the down tube is placed in the DT-HT lug (Figure 7-4). Small gaps are acceptable for this strong, robust joint design. The guideline down the long axis of the DT should align with the point of the lug, if the lug has a point.

Figure 7-4: *A well mitered down tube placed in the HT-DT lug. Note how the miter aligns well with the contours of the lug. The frame builder will likely have to grind out the inside of the lug to get the head tube and down tube to fit. The machine marks on the inside of the lug actually increase the joint surface area, strengthening the joint.*

When the subassembly fits together well, the frame builder should unassembled the subassembly and clean all surfaces as described in Chapter 6, Tip 2. The frame builder should be careful to remove oil residues from the inside of the head tube and down tube and remove the guideline from within five inches of the joint. Oil and ink will burn during brazing, creating oxides.

The frame builder should flux the end of the head tube, down tube, and the inside of the lug as described in Chapter 6, Tip #3. The subassembly should be reassembled carefully with a few millimeters of head tube protruding beyond the bottom of the ring of the lug (Figure 6-1, top left side of the subassembly). After double checking proper fit, the frame builder should place the down tube in the vice and flux the outside of the lug and any tubing within three to four inches of the lug. When brazing this subassembly, the frame builder should use a medium sized flame with the valve regular open about halfway and hold the flame between one and a half to two inches from the steel. If he cannot heat the subassembly to brazing temperature within five minutes, he should open the regulator valve slightly. If the flux starts to turn brown, he should either increase the distance between the torch and steel or close the valve slightly. To ensure good penetration of silver-filler alloy, the frame builder should place the brazing rod at the top of the ring of the lug and move the torch to pull the silver deep to the ring and along the head tube, watching the silver emerge from the bottom of the ring. Likewise, the frame builder should introduce the brazing rod at the edge of the lug along the down tube, and pull the silver through the lug so that it emerges at the head tube (or vice versa).

If necessary, the frame builder can unclamp this subassembly and change its position to provide a better "angle of attack" during any point of the brazing process. However, the frame builder should be careful not to burn himself and must allow the subassembly to cool slightly prior to movement. If the silver alloy is in molten form, gravity may cause the subassembly to fall apart when taken out of the vice. (Any subassembly can be repositioned in this manner during the brazing process). When finished brazing, the frame builder should allow the subassembly to cool and clean it off (as described at the end of Chapter 6).

Mitering the Top Tube

Because the top tube lengths in Table 7-1 are measured center-to-center, these measurements includes part of the seat tube and head tube. The frame builder can estimate the "cut" of the top tube, which is the distance between the center of the miters along the top surface of the tube, by the following formula: TT "cut" = TT (c-c) – ½(ST tube width) – ½(HT tube width). For example, if a frame builder wants to make a 60cm c-c TT with standard-sized tubing, his cut will be 600mm - ½(28.6mm[ST]) – ½(31.7[HT])= 570mm (rounded to the nearest mm) or 57.0cm. This formula explains why the frame builder can build a 670mm long c-c DT with a tube that measures only 650mm in length. Of course, a good math geek can tell you why this formula is an estimate and not an exact calculation. The source of error has something to do with circles verses ovals. However, this estimation method will give the builder a true TT c-c measurement within a few millimeters of the desired measurement.

When the frame builder miters both ends of the top tube, he must be careful not to grind in a miter at one end that is rotated relative to the orientation of the miter at the other end. The guideline drawn along the top surface of the TT helps the frame builder construct well-oriented miters. If, for whatever reason, the frame builder can only make one good miter and one sloppy miter with gaps, (usually because one is rotated relative to the other), he should try to place the good miter in the TT-HT lug because this joint experiences higher stresses than the TT-ST joint.

The frame builder must mark the top tube "cut" estimate upon the top tube. If his measuring tape is not metric, he can covert the estimate to inches (2.54 cm = 1 inch). Basically, the frame builder measures and marks a distance along the TT guideline equal to his cut estimate. Each mark must lie between the transition zone and tube end of both butts.

The frame builder should place the center of each mitering template along the top surface of the top tube. Assuming a classic geometry with 73 degree ST-TT and TT-HT "frame building" angles, the frame builder will enter into tubemiter.exe 107 degrees and 73 degrees for the miters at the ST and HT ends respectively. Of course, the remaining parameters are determined by tube widths and wall thickness. For each template, the frame builder must place a mark as close as possible to the exact center of the middle most miter concavity. The frame builder cuts out his templates, aligns the central mark of each template with the "cut" mark on the long-axis guideline of the TT, secures the miters in place, and grinds in the miters (figure 7-5). The frame builder should mark the ends of the top tube "ST" and "HT" appropriately.

Figure 7-5: *A pre-cut top tube with miter templates secured at each end. The frame builder must make sure that the entire miter-end of each template is located within the thick-butted zone of the tube end. The frame builder avoids grinding in miters that are rotated relative to each other by lining up a mark in the center of the template with the long-axis guideline of the top tube.*

Preparing the Seat Tube-Bottom Bracket Shell Subassembly

The miter for the ST-BB joint is a compound miter because the ST intersects both the BB and the DT. This miter, however, is very easy to make and does not require a paper template. Prior to mitering, the builder must grind out the inside of the ST lug of the BB shell until the butted end of the seat tube fits into the lug. Once the ST is in place, the builder can simply draw in the miter. He can access the ST through the holes in the BB shell for the DT and BB cartridge and use a marker to trace in the contours of the BB onto the ST (Figure 7-6). The frame builder then cuts and grinds in this miter but SHOULD NOT braze the ST-BB assembly yet (Figure 7-7).

Figure 7-6: *To prepare for a miter, the frame builder can trace the contours of the bottom bracket shell onto the butted end of the seat tube.*

Figure 7-7: *Final miter for the seat-tube-bottom-bracket-shell subassembly.*

Preparing the Seat Tube-Top Tube Subassembly

To finish the preparation of the ST, frame builder should place the mitered end of the ST into the BB shell and align the miter with the contours with the shell. He should place the end of the tape measure at the center of the BB shell (the future location of the BB spindle) and measure and mark the desired ST center-to-center length (Table 7-1) on the side of the seat tube. He should place the ST-TT lug next to the ST, align the center of the lug with the measurement mark, and mark the estimated location of the top of the ST-TT lug on the ST (Figure 7-8). Some cast ST-TT lugs have a lip at the top of the lug that prevents the ST from passing all the way through the lug. If the frame builder has this type of lug, he will need to cut the seat tube off at the estimated top location of the ST-TT lug, and grind the top of the tube so that the top of the ST lies flush with the lip of the ST-TT lug.

64

Figure 7-8: *Marking measurements on the seat tube. The mark already present on the tube is the top of the center-to-center seat tube measurement measured from the middle of the bottom bracket shell. The location of the magic marker estimates the location of the top of the ST-TT lug. If the ST-TT lug design does not allow the seat tube to pass all the way through the lug, the frame builder will need to cut the tube off at this location.*

Marking the Remainder of the Front Triangle

The frame builder needs to make several more marks and measurements before he can complete the front triangle. The frame builder should place the ST into the BB shell and align the miter appropriately. He should place the un-mitered end (the long butt) of the down tube-head tube subassembly into the down tube lug of the bottom bracket shell and rotate the down tube in the lug until the head tube appears to lie in the same plane as the seat tube. The guideline down the long-axis of the DT should align with the point of the lug of the BB shell, if there is a point. He should carefully place the three assembled tubes on a level surface, align the ST miter of the TT with the c-c mark of the seat tube and lay the TT in place (Figure 7-9). The frame builder will have to move the DT back and forth within the BB down tube lug to get the TT to bridge the ST and HT appropriately. The mitered ends of the TT should lie against the ST and HT with minimal gapping. If necessary, the frame builder may need to cut a few inches off the long butt of the DT if the DT touches the far side of the BB shell before the TT can form a bridge. The frame builder should cut off as little tube as possible and make sure this cut does not extend beyond the thick butt. When the TT bridges the ST and HT correctly, the frame builder should double check that the ST lies parallel to the HT and that the ST and HT lie in the same plane. If necessary, the frame builder may need to make adjustments, rotating the DT in the BB shell.

Figure 7-9: *The frame builder aligns all the tubes of the front triangle. Note how the down tube protrudes into the body of the bottom bracket shell. If necessary, the frame builder may have to make a cut at this end of the DT to allow the TT to bridge the ST and DT. The frame builder should rotate the DT within the BB shell until the HT and ST lie in the same plane. The frame builder makes c-c measurements of the HT, DT, ST, and TT. If the measurements are correct, he finishes marking the frame.*

The frame builder should measure the c-c lengths of the DT, TT, HT, and ST (Figure 7-9). These real measurements should be within a few millimeters of the desired lengths. If one or more of the measurements is off by more than a centimeter, the frame builder will need to figure out what went wrong, un-assembling and reassembling the frame if necessary.

When the measurements are acceptable to the frame builder, he makes three marks: The first mark locates the top of the ST-TT joint; the frame builder uses a marker to trace the top curve of the TT onto the front of the ST. The second mark locates the top of the HT-TT joint; the frame builder traces the top curve of the TT onto the backside of the HT. The third mark locates the end of the DT within the BB shell; the frame builder traces the contour of the near side of the inside of the BB shell onto the DT (Figure 7-10). Being careful not to rotate the BB shell upon the DT, the frame builder removes the TT from the HT and ST, and removes the ST from the BB shell. The frame builder can now finish tracing the remainder of the DT miter curve onto the DT using a similar method used to trace the ST miter (discussed above).

Figure 7-10: *With all tubes of the front triangle in place, and the ST in the same plane as the HT, the frame builder traces the contours of the inside of the bottom bracket shell onto the DT. The frame builder will need to remove the ST from the BB shell to finish tracing the DT miter.*

Finishing the Subassemblies

The frame builder should grind in the miter traced onto the long butt of the DT. However, the frame builder should stop when he has a good course miter and not waste too much time completing a fine miter for reasons discussed later.

The frame builder should clean the outside and inside of the ST and BB shell. He should flux the outside of the ST and the inside of the entire BB shell and assemble the subassembly, making sure not to place the ST into the DT lug of the BB shell by mistake. In the presence of flux, which obscures the frame builder's view, the frame builder will need to feel the inside of the BB shell to make sure the miter is in the correct place. The frame builder needs to place the non-butted end of the seat tube into the vice so that the BB shell faces skyward (Figure 7-11). Using a protractor placed against the side of the seat tube, the frame builder should ensure that the seat tube is perpendicular to the ground (gravity), adjusting the position of the seat tube within the vice if necessary (Figure 7-11). The frame builder should place the protractor on top of the bottom bracket shell, making sure the long axis of the BB shell is parallel to the ground and perpendicular to the ST. Once the subassembly is properly aligned, the frame builder can flux the outside of the BB shell (Figure 6-2).

Figure 7-11: *Prior to brazing, the frame builder uses a protractor to makes sure the long axis of the ST is perpendicular to the ground and the long axis of the BB shell is perpendicular to the ST (not shown).*

When the frame builder brazes the BB-ST joint, he will need to use more heat output than he did for the HT-DT subassembly. He should introduce the silver at the edge of the lug at the bottom of the joint, drawing the silver upward against gravity. To ensure good penetration of silver, the frame builder needs to see silver alloy emerge between the mitered end of the tube and the contours inside of the BB shell. If necessary, the frame builder may have to place the end of the torch or the brazing rod but never both at the same time on the inside of the BB shell. Because the ST-BB joint is a high stress joint, the novice frame builder may need to use a large amount of flux and slightly overheat the subassembly if necessary. Unsightly globs of silver in the wrong location are better than a poorly penetrated, weak joint. When finished brazing, the frame builder should cool and clean the subassembly. Being careful not to score the BB threads, the builder may use a rotary tool to grind down any lips of the ST that protrude beyond the contours of the inside of the BB. At this point, the frame builder should not worry about silver that bonds to the threads of the BB shell.

The frame builder should grind out the inside of the ST-TT lug and the ST-HT lugs until the tubes fit into the lugs properly. The frame builder should place the ST-TT lug on the end of the ST, aligning the top contour of the TT portion of the lug with the bottom of the TT guide contour that was traced upon the ST. If the frame builder has not cut down the top of the ST, he should trace the top of the ST-TT lug upon the ST. If he already cut off the top of the ST, he merely needs to makes sure the ST-TT fits well.

The frame builder should place the HT-TT lug on the HT, aligning the top contour of the TT potion of the lug with the bottom of the TT contour that was traced onto the back of the HT. The frame builder should trace the top of the HT-TT lug ring onto the HT, and he should mark a dot on the HT that is centered within the TT portion of the lug (Figure 7-12). This dot represents the future location of the hot gas vent. The frame builder should remove the lug and drill in the vent using the method described in Chapter 5 (Figures 5-9 and 5-10).

Figure 7-12: *The frame builder places the HT-TT lug on the HT, marks the location of the top of the lug onto the HT, and places a dot at a central location within the TT potion of the lug. This dot marks the location of the hot gas vent.*

Finishing the Front Triangle

The frame builder is now ready to reassemble and finish brazing the front triangle. The frame builder must thoroughly clean the ST-TT and TT-HT lugs, both ends of the TT, the mitered end of the DT, and the inside and outside of the BB shell. When the frame builder cleans the top of the ST and HT, he should leave a trace amount of ink behind so that he can barely see the marks that locate the top of the lugs. Although this ink will burn and create oxides during the brazing process, the flux should be able to handle the contamination provided the rest of the joint is clean.

Prior to assembly, the frame builder should apply flux to the mitered end of the DT, both ends of the TT, the inside of the BB shell and the inside of the two remaining lugs. He applies flux only downward from the lug-ring marks on the HT and ST.

To preassemble the frame, the frame builder should place the HT-TT lug on the HT and the ST-TT lug on the ST, aligning the top of the lugs with the (barely visible) marks. The frame builder should place the appropriate end of the TT into the ST-TT lug, and clamp the DT into the vice (Figure 7-13).

Figure 7-13: *Final assembly of the front triangle. The frame builder places the DT in the vice. The TT is connected (by friction) to the ST by the ST-TT lug (background).*

For final assembly, the frame builder picks up the ST-BB-TT subassembly. Holding the TT in place in the ST-TT lug, the frame builder simultaneously inserts the mitered end of the DT into the lug of the BB shell and the HT end of the TT into the HT-TT lug. This task is tricky and may require the help of an assistant. When fully assembled by friction (Figure 7-14), the frame builder should rotate the ST-BB subassembly upon the mitered end of the DT so that the ST appears to lie in the same plane as the HT. The frame builder should re-measure the center-to-center distances of the HT, DT, ST, and TT to make sure the frame is assembled properly and should make adjustments if necessary. The frame builder needs to look inside the bottom bracket shell to see if the mitered end of the DT lies flush with the contours of the BB shell. A DT, a few millimeters short or long relative to these contours, is acceptable, (hence the need for only a rough miter). If the assembly is acceptable to the frame builder he fluxes the outside of the joints to be brazed.

Figure 7-14: *The front triangle fully assembled by friction. Prior to brazing, the frame builder needs to double check all center-to-center measurements, double check the alignment (discussed below), and flux the outer surfaces of the lugs.*

The last step, before brazing, is to double check the alignment of the front triangle. The frame builder moves the DT in the vice so that the HT appears to lie perpendicular to the ground. Using a protractor, the frame builder adjusts the position of the down tube until the measured angle does in fact indicate that the head tube is perpendicular to the ground (Figure 7-15). When the correct orientation is achieved, the DT is clamped down securely in the vice so that the DT-HT subassembly will not move with an accidental bump. Next the frame builder places the protractor against the side of the seat tube and rotates the ST-BB-TT subassembly upon the DT until the ST is perpendicular to the ground and parallel to the HT (Figure 7-16). The frame builder removes the protractor and peers down the top tube, as if the ST and HT were the back and front sights of a rifle. The overall appearance of the front triangle and the protractor measurements should tell the frame builder the same story; that the entire front triangle lies in the same plane, with the ST parallel to the HT. If something is amiss, the frame builder needs to make corrections prior to proceeding.

When absolutely convinced that the front triangle is aligned, the frame builder should tack the point of the DT lug of the BB shell to the top surface of the DT by brazing the two parts together with a small amount of silver. The tack should be about 5mm in diameter. The frame builder repeats the angle measurements of the HT and ST relative to gravity, and if all is well, he can proceed to final brazing.

Figure 7-15: *The frame builder uses a protractor to align the head tube perpendicular to the ground and clamps the DT-HT subassembly securely in place.*

Figure 7-16: *The frame builder uses a protractor to make sure that the ST is parallel to the HT and the entire front triangle lies in a single plane perpendicular to the ground.*

Of the joints that remain to be brazed, the DT-BB joint should be brazed first. The method used to braze this joint is nearly identical to that used to braze the ST-BB joint. The only difference is that the frame builder must start brazing on the bottom side of the DT, opposite the tack. Otherwise, the tack may melt, the BB shell may rotate on the DT, and the frame builder looses his good alignment. As with the ST-BB joint, the frame builder may need to place the flame or brazing rod (but never both) inside the BB shell to ensure good penetration of filler metal.

The method to braze the HT-TT joint is no different than that of the HT-DT joint. If the frame builder has a ST-TT lug that allows the ST to completely pass through the lug (e.g. no lip), then the ST-TT joint is brazed in the same manner as the HT-TT and HT-DT joint. If the ST-TT lug has a lip, (requiring the frame builder to cut the ST to size prior to assembly), the ST-TT joint is brazed somewhat differently. In this case, the frame builder will need to peer into the inside of the ST, making sure the silver penetrates underneath and deep to the lip of the lug. The frame builder may need to place the flame or brazing rod (but never both at the same time) into the ST.

After brazing all joints, the frame builder should cool and clean the front triangle. If necessary, he should use a rotary tool or file to grind off any lips of the DT that protrude beyond the contours of the BB shell. As with the ST-BB subassembly, the frame builder must be careful not to score the BB threads and need not worry about any silver that bonded to the threads.

Chapter 8: The Rear Triangle

Goals and Objectives

Putting together the rear triangle, so that the rear wheel is centered in the stays and lies in the same plane as the front triangle, is by far the most difficult task for the first time frame builder. However, once the chainstays are brazed into the exact location, the remainder of the build is pretty easy. Getting the chainstays brazed in just right can be a major source of frustration. If one chainstay is only a few millimeters longer or higher than the other, rear wheel alignment will be terrible. Professional frame builders use jigs that weigh hundreds of pounds and cost thousands of dollars to eliminate this very problem. Through trial and error, I managed to figure out a rear triangle building method that circumvents the need for an expensive jig. The method I present is simple and effective but so amateurish that it probably makes professional frame builders cuss or cringe. The key is to tack down the chainstays with the rear wheel in place.

The first time frame builder should not attempt to bend the chainstay sockets of the bottom bracket shell, (a skill necessary to create clearance for fat mountain bike tires). Even a slight discrepancy between the orientation of the two sockets will make obtaining good rear triangle alignment extremely difficult. The first time frame builder simply does not possess the skills and technique needed to bend the sockets evenly.

Horizontal dropouts, on the other hand, create a fair amount of latitude in obtaining proper rear triangle alignment. The rider can rotate the orientation of the rear wheel axle in these types of drops to compensate for small discrepancies in chainstay length. However, the frame builder will still need to place the chainstays in the same plane so that one dropout is not higher than the other. If the frame builder obtains articulated horizontal dropouts, he should follow the directions for rear triangle alignment presented in this manual, pressing the wheel axle as deep as possible into the dropouts.

The ideal rear triangle build places the rim equidistant between chainstays and seatstays and in the same plane as the front triangle. A rim slightly closer to stays on one side of the bike (left versus right) but in a plane parallel to the front triangle is acceptable as long as the stays allow clearance for the desired tire. Many production bicycles are aligned this way as "within acceptable tolerances." The first time builder, however, should only accept this outcome after several failed attempts at better alignment.

If the rim is centered in the chainstays but not in the seatstays, the wheel generally lies in a plane that is rotated relative to the plane of the front triangle. Though less than ideal, this outcome is acceptable if the stays allow for adequate tire clearance.

An important pitfall to avoid is the creation of a rear triangle where the wheel is centered in both the chainstays and seatstays but does not lie in the same plane as the front triangle. This outcome is unacceptable and frequently occurs after ill-fated attempts to bend the chainstay sockets of the bottom bracket shell.

Seat Stay-Partial Dropout Subassemblies

Each dropout of the vertical dropout set recommended for this manual comes in two pieces: a large piece that contains the drop itself and a small articulating lug for the seat stay (Figure 4-2). In this manual, to minimize confusion, I will refer to the larger piece as the "dropout" and the smaller piece as the "partial dropout."

The seatstay-partial dropout subassemblies are probably the easiest subassemblies to construct. The frame builder should use a small grinding bit on his rotary tool to grind out the seatstay socket of the partial dropout until the stay fits snugly. If the fit is loose, the frame builder can bend down the points of the lug with vice grips to eliminate slop. The partial dropouts and seatstays should be thoroughly cleaned prior to brazing.

Round seatstays possess radial symmetry along the long axis, so the frame builder need not worry about misaligning the partial dropout lug on the stay. The frame builder should flux the entire inside and outside of the dropout lug. Failure to flux the articulating portion of the partial dropout will result in the accumulation of oxides directly on the steel surface during brazing. These oxides are very difficult to remove and will result in a weak braze when this seatstay subassembly is brazed into the remainder of the dropout.

Because this subassembly is relatively small, the frame builder should use a smaller flame than for the joints of the front triangle. The flame builder should point the flame at the articulating lug, which heats up slowly compared to the seatstay (Figure 8-1). If the frame builder points the flame at the seatstay, the seatstay will reach brazing temperature faster than the lug, and the frame builder risks creating a silver-tipped stay, with no silver actually bonding to the partial dropout. The frame builder should observe silver bonding to both the stay and the lug to ensure a good braze. I recommend the frame builder introduce the silver at the concave portions of each side of the lug, moving the flame to pull silver around the sides and down the points. After cooling, the frame builder should place the dropout end of the subassembly in a bucket of water to remove the flux. If water penetrates into the inside of the seatstays, then there is a void in the braze and the frame builder will need to reflux and re-braze the subassembly.

Figure 8-1: *Brazing the seatstay-partial dropout subassembly, (normally there are only two per a frame). The frame builder should point the flame at the partial dropout and use a liberal amount of flux.*

Building the Chainstay-Dropout Subassemblies

Building the chainstay-dropout subassemblies follows a procedure nearly identical to that used for the seatstay-parital dropout subassembly. For completely round tapered chainstays, the frame builder does not need to worry about orientation of the dropout upon the chainstay because the chainstay possesses radial symmetry.

For oval-round chainstays or round-oval-round chainstays, the frame builder must align the plane of the dropout with the long axis of the cross section of the oval. The frame builder can place the oval end in the vice and align the dropout as best he can by "eyeballing it."

Alternatively, for oval-round chainstays (but not round-oval-round chainstays), the builder can place the oval end of the stay in the chainstay socket of the bottom bracket shell. A protractor is used to align the plane of the dropout with the short axis (the circular edges) of the bottom bracket shell. When properly aligned both structures should be perpendicular to the ground.

78

Grinding and fluxing the chainstay-dropout subassembly follows the same method used for the seatstay-partial dropout subassembly. The frame builder must flux the entire outer surface of the dropout, point the fame at the dropout (Figure 6-5), and make sure the silver bonds to both the dropout and the stay. During cleaning, if water penetrates the insides of the chainstays, the builder will have to reflux and rebraze the subassembly.

Estimating Chainstay Length

Most uncut chainstays are longer than 400mm, and the frame builder will likely need to cut the chainstays down to size. Otherwise, the constructed frame, although functional, will have a large ugly gap between the rear wheel and the seat tube. In this manual, we do not use trigonometric functions to arrive at precise calculations for chainstay length. Rather, we estimate chainstay length simply and qualitatively.

The frame builder should place the front triangle upon a level surface with the drive side (right side) facing up. He should place the rear wheel with the desired fully inflated tire behind the front triangle, leaving the desired gap between the wheel and seat tube. Generally this gap is small for road racing frames with thin tires and tight handling characteristics and bigger for touring and cyclocross bicycles with fatter tires and more stable handling. The frame builder should place the rear axle of the wheel in the dropout of the drive side chainstay, (which has a deraillier hanger), and place the opposite end of the chainstay along the side of the bottom bracket shell. The framebuilder should move the wheel up or down to make sure the long axis of the chainstay aligns with the orientation of the BB shell chainstay socket (Figure 8-2).

Figure 8-2: *Aligning the rear wheel, front triangle, and chainstay-dropout subassembly. The frame builder must pay close attention to the orientation of the long axis of the chainstay and the gap between the wheel and seat tube. The frame builder does not need to have a cassette for this procedure but should include the desired, fully inflated tire.*

When the rear wheel, front triangle and the chainstay are in the correct desired location and orientation, the frame builder should mark on the chainstay, the approximate location of the outermost edge of the tire and the innermost location of the chainstay socket of the bottom bracket shell (Figure 8-3).

Figure 8-3: *The frame builder should mark on the chainstay, the outermost location of the tire and the innermost location of the socket of the bottom bracket shell.*

The frame builder should put the chainstay in the vice and make a cut between the socket guideline and the open end of the chainstay. This cut should be at least ½" from the line to guarantee the chainstays are not cut too short. After making this cut, the frame builder should align the uncut chainstay with to the cut chainstay, and mark the length of the shorter chainstay upon the longer one. The longer chainstay should be cut at this mark. At this point, the frame builder should not worry if one chainstay is longer than the other by a few millimeters as long as neither is too short.

Final Preparation of the Chainstay Subassemblies

Prior to brazing the chainstays into the BB shell, the frame builder needs to miter the chainstays and bend the dropouts to the proper orientation. Both these tasks need to be performed diligently.

The frame builder should grind out the inside of the chainstay sockets of the bottom bracket shell, removing all oxides and making sure the chainstays can fit all the way through (Figure 8-4). For oval chainstay sockets, the frame builder may need to use a narrow grinding bit along the top and bottom of the socket.

Figure 8-4: *The frame builder should grind out the sockets of the BB shell until the chainstays can fit all the way through. The frame builder will miter the stays later so that there is room in the shell for the bottom bracket cartridge.*

The frame builder should place the down tube snugly in the vice, the chainstays in the sockets of the BB shell, and the rear wheel in the dropout (Figure 8-5). At this point, the frame builder should make sure his wheel is true and make adjustments if necessary. The frame builder will not be able to use his wheel as a frame-alignment tool if the rim does not lie in a single plane.

Figure 8-5: *Assembly of the front triangle, chainstay subassemblies, and rear wheel. The rear wheel must be true.*

The frame builder should inspect the location of the outer sides of the tire relative to the inner surfaces of the chainstays. If the tire is closer to one chainstay than the other, he needs to either shorten (push in) the chainstay closest to the tire or lengthen (pull out) the chainstay farther from the tire (Figure 8-6, top). To push the chainstay further into the bottom bracket shell, the frame builder can tap very lightly with a hammer or mallet on the end of the dropout. The frame builder should not perform this task with force or the dropout will bend or deform. If more than a light tap is needed to push the chainstay forward, the frame builder should grind out more metal from the chainstay socket of the bottom bracket shell to loosen the fit. To pull a chainstay a small distance out of the socket, the frame builder can lightly tap the part of the dropout that articulates with the seatstay subassembly. The direction of the hammer tap is, of course, away from the front triangle. The frame builder should lengthen and shorten the stays until the rim and tire is centered in the chainstays with the correct gap between tire and seat tube (Figure 8-6, bottom).

84

Figure 8-6: *View of the wheel from below the bicycle. Top: the chainstay on the left is too long, causing the tire and rim to lie too close to the left chainstay. Bottom: After pushing the left chainstay into the bottom bracket shell a few millimeters, the rim and wheel are well centered in the chainstays. (The astute frame builder may notice the gaps between the points of the sockets and the sides of the chainstay. The oval section of this round-oval-round chainstay causes this gap. The author later rounded the oval section in a vice eliminating this gap. Round-oval-round chainstays are not recommended for the first time frame builder).*

When the rear wheel is well centered in the chainstays, the frame builder should mark the location of the socket point on the side of the chainstay to use as a reference later (Figure 8-7). If the socket does not have a point, the frame builder should mark the location of the approximate center of the socket.

Figure 8-7: *Reference mark on the chainstays. The frame builder makes this mark after centering the wheel in the chainstays.*

The frame builder should look at the dropout and determine how the plane of the dropout lies relative to the wheel axle. In most cases, this plane will not lie perpendicular to the axle (which is the desired configuration). The gap between the dropout and inner spacer of the axle tells the frame builder how he needs to bend the dropout. If the gap between the spacer and dropout is at the rear of the dropout, the angle between the dropout and chainstay is too obtuse (Figure 8-8). The frame builder would need to bend the end of the dropout toward the midline (wheel) of the bicycle. If the gap occurs at the front of the dropout, the angle is too small. The frame builder would need to bend the dropout away from the midline.

Figure 8-8: *A small gap between the inner spacer of the wheel axle and the very rear of the dropout indicates that the angle between the chainstay and dropout is too obtuse.*

Bending the dropout is not a delicate procedure. The frame builder should place the chainstay subassembly in the dropout so that the entire flat surface of the dropout slot touch the vice jaws (Figure 8-9). If part of the slot is above or below the jaws, the frame builder will place a bend through the slot, and the slot will not lie in a single plane, which is undesirable. To make the bend, the frame builder grabs the very end of the chainstay and simply pulls or pushes to make the bend in the appropriate direction (Figure 8-9). If the subassembly is secured correctly in the vice and well brazed, the bend will occur in the desired location, which is between the end of the chainstay and the slot. If the chainstay pops out of its lug in the dropout, the subassembly was poorly brazed. The frame builder will have to examine the inside of the lug to figure out what went wrong. The likely culprit is either poor penetration of the silver (resulting in voids) or inadequate heat (causing the silver to bond to either just the stay or the dropout but not both). The builder should reshape any bent steel, clean, reflux and rebraze the subassembly.

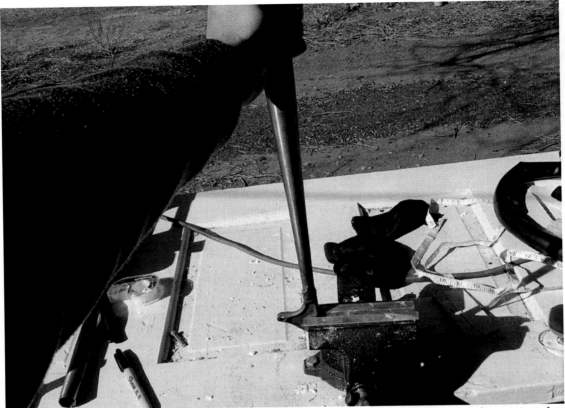

Figure 8-9: *Bending the dropout. The frame builder needs to make sure the entire slot lies in the vice jaws so that the bend will occur between the slot and chainstay. The chainstay will not pop out of the dropout if the subassembly was brazed properly.*

Assuming the bend went well, the frame builder should repeat the bending process with the other chainstay. After placing the chainstays back into their sockets and aligning the marks on the side of the stays with the points of the sockets, the builder should reassess the orientation of the dropout relative to the wheel axle. If necessary, he may need to make additional corrective bends until the dropout slot lies flush against the spacer (figure 8-10).

Figure 8-10: *Proper alignment of the dropout. The flat surface of the dropout slot lies flush with the inner spacer of the wheel axle.*

At this point, with the correct bend in the stays, the frame builder should reassess the alignment of his rear wheel. He may need to push in or pull out the chainstays slightly to compensate for the new bends in the dropouts. Quantitatively, the frame builder should verify wheel alignment by measuring the distance between each side of the rim and top of the adjacent chainstay with a tape measure (Figure 8-11). These two measurements will be equal for a well aligned rear triangle. The frame builder should adjust the stays if necessary.

Figure 8-11: *Using a tape measure to verify that the wheel is centered in the chainstays.*

When the wheel is centered, the frame builder should trace the curve of the inner surface of the bottom bracket shell onto the outer side of each chainstay (Figure 8-12). With each chainstay marked, the frame builder should remove the wheel and one of the two chainstays. The frame builder can now access and trace the inner curve of the bottom bracket shell onto the inside of the chainstay (Figure 8-13). If the frame builder's marker is not long enough to reach inside the bottom bracket shell, he may use a scratch awl. The frame builder can remove the completely marked chainstay, and insert the chainstay that was previously removed. He should align the traced mark with the bottom bracket shell, and trace the curve of the BB shell onto the inside of this stay.

Figure 8-12: *Using a marker to trace the inner curve of the bottom bracket shell onto the outer sides of the chainstays. The frame builder should verify that the wheel is centered in the stays before performing this task.*

Figure 8-13: *By removing the near chainstay, the frame builder can access the far end of the inside of the BB shell and trace the inner curve of the BB shell onto the inside of the chainstay.*

The frame builder now has a curve on the inside and outside of each chainstay for a miter. At this point the frame builder should grind in a rough miter (Figure 8-14). A fine miter is not necessary.

Figure 8-14: *Appearance of the chainstay with a rough miter.*

Brazing in the Chainstays

Because we tack down the chainstays with the rear wheel in place, I recommend the first time builder acquire a cheap rear wheel that is true and that has the same axle width and rim diameter as the wheel he wishes to use on the final bicycle. The wheel is exposed to heat during the tacking process, so using a high quality wheel can be an expensive mistake. Ideally, the frame builder should pick up a cheap set of steel rimmed wheels at a yard sale and either add or remove spacers to arrive at the correct axle length. Compared to steel, aluminum has a very low melting point and easily distorts in the presence of heat. (I will discuss an alternative to tacking down the stays with the wheel in place later on).

Prior to reassembly and brazing, the frame builder needs to thoroughly clean the bottom bracket shell and the mitered ends of the chainstays. All guide marks should be removed with mineral spirits. The frame builder should liberally flux the chainstays and bottom bracket shell. The chainstays should be inserted into the sockets so that the mitered end is flush with the inner contours of the bottom bracket shell. The cheap, true wheel should be placed in the drops, and the frame builder should push in or pull out the chainstays until the wheel is centered. At this point, the frame builder may discover that one chainstay may either protrude slightly into the bottom bracket shell or not completely protrude through the lug.

The frame builder should not worry about un-flush mitered chainstays as long as the distance from ideal flush fit is small, less than a few millimeters. The frame builder should not grind off any protruding chainstay lips due to their proximity to the BB threads. I will discuss how to deal with this situation later.

Prior to brazing, the frame builder needs to make sure the rear wheel will be centered in the seatstays. He should place the articulating ends of the seatstays into the corresponding sockets of the dropouts, lie the other end of the seatstays against the ST-TT lug, and secure the ends in place with a piece of brake cable and vice grips (Figure 8-15). If the seatstays are very long, the ends may touch each other, preventing the frame builder from laying them against the ST-TT lug. If this occurs, the frame builder should lay the seatstay ends further on down the TT. For the purposes of centering the wheel, the exact location of the seatstays is unimportant provided they lie at the same point along the long axis of the TT.

Figure 8-15: *Using a brake cable and vice grips to secure the seatstays against the ST-TT lug.*

To determine if the rear wheel is centered in the seatstays, the frame builder should look at the frame and rear wheel from behind (Figure 8-16). If the wheel is closer to one seatstay than another, then the dropouts' heights are uneven relative to the axis of the seat tube. The frame builder will need to either raise the dropout of the seatstay closest to the wheel, or lower the dropout on the other side. The frame builder either pushes up or pulls down on the dropout but should not push the chainstay into or out of its socket.

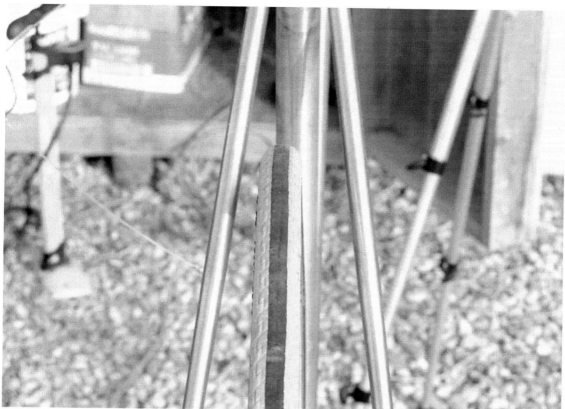

Figure 8-16: *The wheel is not centered in the seatstays. The dropout on the left is lower (relative to the axis of the seat tube) than the right dropout. The frame builder will either have to pull up on the left dropout or down on the right to center the wheel.*

Another clue to wheel alignment lies in the examination of the ends of the seatstays. The tops of the seatstays should be even when the wheel is centered (Figure 8-17).

Figure 8-17: *Uneven tops of the seatstays. Provided the seatstays are the same length, the tops of the seatstays will be even when the wheel is centered. In this case, the dropout on the left is too low, and the wheel is consequently too close to the left seatstay.*

Prior to tacking down the chainstays, four additional measurements are needed: 1. The frame builder should re-measure the distance from the top of each chainstay to the adjacent side of the rim to make sure the wheel is centered in the chainstays (Figure 8-11); 2. The frame builder needs to measure the distance from the top surface of each seatstay to the adjacent side of the rim to make sure the wheel is centered in the seatstays (Figure 8-18); 3. The frame builder needs to place a protractor on the side of the rim and the side of the seat tube to make sure the plane of the wheel is not rotated relative to the plane of the front triangle (Figure 8-19); and 4. The frame builder needs to examine the frame and wheel from above to make sure the rear wheel indeed lies in the same plane as the front triangle. This last estimate is very important because measurements #1 through #3 above may give the desired results but the plane of the rear wheel may still be tilted relative to the plane of the front triangle.

Figure 8-18: *Measuring the distance from each seatstay to the rim to make sure the wheel is centered in the seatstays.*

Figure 8-19: *Placing the protractor on the side of the seat tube (top), and rim (bottom) to make sure the plane of the wheel is not rotated relative to the plan of the front triangle. With good alignment, the protractor should give the same reading with both measurements.*

Tacking is simply the act of making a very small braze. Once the frame builder is absolutely convinced that his rear wheel is centered, he should tack down the top of the chainstay in the socket. Unlike for all other brazing, the frame builder should not move the torch, but simply point from the back downward toward the front to avoid averting heat to the wheel (Figure 8-20). The frame builder needs to introduce just enough filler material between the top of the chainstay and socket to prevent the chainstay from moving or wiggling around. He does not need to worry about good penetration at this time. Both chainstays need to be tacked in place.

(Alternatively, the frame builder can skip the task of tacking down the chainstays with the rear wheel in place. Rather, he can make a series of marks on the chainstays and chainstay sockets to use as a reference. He measures the lengths of the chainstays from socket to dropout, the lengths of the seatstays from TT to dropout, and the angles of the chainstays and seatstays relative to gravity. He disassembles the rear triangle, removing the rear wheel, and reassembles the rear triangle with the jig discussed below. He lines up the marks on the chainstays and sockets and makes sure the chainstay and seatstay lengths and angles are preserved. If all marks and measurements are correct, he brazes the chainstays in place and hopes for the best. I have used this method myself and found it to yield less predictable alignment than tacking down the chainstays with the rear wheel in place).

Figure 8-20: *Tacking the chainstays in place. The frame builder makes a small braze, introducing filler material between the top of the chainstay and its socket. The frame builder must be careful to direct the flame towards the front or he will destroy the wheel.*

As the tack cools, the frame builder should construct a jig for the rear triangle. He should use his 3/8" bolts and nuts to bolt his two strips of angle steel together so that they are parallel and 1 1/8" apart. This distance corresponds to the tube width of the ST and TT for oversized frames and the ST and DT of standard sized frames. The frame builder should place the threaded rod through the holes at the very end of the angle steel, securing them in place with nuts (Figure 8-21). The threaded rod takes the place of the wheel axle, and nuts take the place of axle spacers. If the frame builder wishes to use a road hub, the outermost surface of these "spacers" need to be 130mm apart and centered about the middle of the jig. For mountain hubs, the spacers should be 135mm apart. Some manufacturers of cyclocross bikes space their dropouts 132.5mm apart to accommodate both mountain and road hubs. All nuts of the jig should be tightened to make the jig as stiff as possible.

The frame builder should turn the frame upside down, clamping the top tube in the vice at a location near the seat tube. The jig is easier to insert and remove when the frame is in this position. The threaded rod is placed in the dropouts so that the spacer nuts touch the inside of the drops. For a standard sized frame, the frame builder uses two C clamps to clamp the angle steel against the seat tube and the down tube (Figure 8-21). For oversized frames, the jig is clamped against the seat tube and top tube. The frame builder should secure the jig in the dropouts with a final pair of nuts.

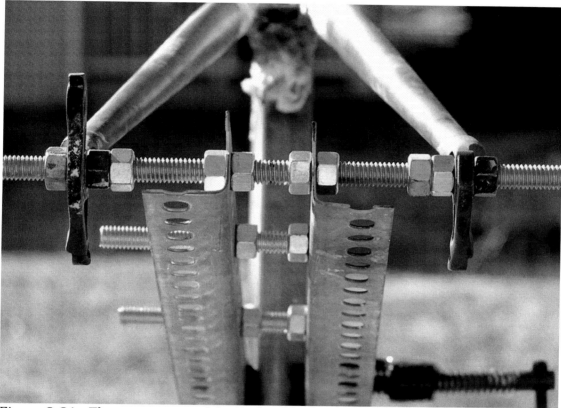

Figure 8-21: *The appearance of the jig for the rear triangle. The inner surfaces of the two strips of angle steel should be 1 1/8" apart, and the inner surfaces of the nuts just interior to the dropouts should be at a distance corresponding to the length of the desired wheel axle.*

When the dropouts are secure in the jig, the frame builder can braze the chainstays into the sockets of the bottom bracket shell. For each chainstay, the builder should start brazing on the side opposite the tack. Melting the tack before laying down more filler material may cause the chainstays to move. To ensure good penetration, the frame builder should point the flame at the sockets of the bottom bracket shell and draw the silver alloy all the way through the socket (Figure 8-22). He should be able to see filler emerge into the inside of the BB shell from between the socket and stay. The frame builder may need to place the brazing rod or flame but never both at the same time inside the BB shell to ensure adequate penetration of filler alloy. Silver that bonds to the threads of the BB shell is of little consequence. We will discuss what to do about this situation later.

When all brazing is complete, the frame builder should allow the frame to cool, remove the jig, and return the wheel to the drops. If the frame builder made a good tack that did not allow the chainstays to move or wiggle and if he made the jig properly, the wheel should be centered. If not, the frame builder will need to heat and un-braze one of the chainstays and try again. To un-braze the chainstay, the frame builder should put the frame in the vice so that the dropouts point toward the ground. A 5+ lbs weight should be secured to the dropout of the chainstay with a section of brake cable. The frame builder should heat the BB chainstay socket using the largest flame possible and move the flame constantly and systematically so all filler material will melt at roughly the same time. The traction on the chainstay will cause it to pop out of the socket.

Figure 8-22: *Brazing the chainstays in place. The frame builder should start on the side opposite the tack and point the flame at the socket.*

(As an alternative to building a jig for the rear triangle, the frame builder can simply braze in the chainstays with the rear wheel in place. Of course, the frame builder is much more likely to destroy his rear wheel with heat. I have used this method myself, and I find it yields less predictable alignment than constructing the jig).

Final Preparation of Seatstay Subassemblies

Prior to completing the rear triangle, the frame builder needs to cut the seatstays to size and braze on seatstay caps, drilling hot air vents if necessary. Some seatstay caps are manufactured with vent holes, which will save the frame builder a little work (Figure 8-23).

Figure 8-23: *Seatstay caps, front view (top), and back view (bottom). This pair comes with vent holes pre-drilled in the back, so the frame builder will not have to drill hot gas vent holes in the seatstays.*

The builder should put the wheel in the drops and place the articulated end of the seatstay subassemblies in the dropouts. If the wheel is not centered in the seatstays, the frame builder will have to un-braze one of the chainstays and re-braze it to obtain proper alignment. Assuming the wheel is well centered, the frame builder should lay the top of the seatstay subassembly against the ST-TT lug and mark on the seatstay the topmost intersection of the seatstay and the lug (Figure 8-24). This line represents the future location of the top of seatstay cap on the final subassembly.

Figure 8-24: *The frame builder marks on the seatstay where the top of the seatstay cap will lie against the ST-TT lug.*

To measure where to cut the seatstay, the frame builder should place the seatstay on a flat surface and place the seatstay cap next to the seatstay so that the top of the cap lines up with the builder's guideline. The frame builder should mark the location of the top of the seatstay cap plug on the seatstay (Figure 8-25). The seatstay is secured in the vice, and the frame builder should cut off the excess steel at the plug line. This cut should be made as perpendicular as possible to the long axis of the seatstay. Once this cut is made, the frame builder should place the short cut seatstay against the long uncut seatstay, lining up the two dropout ends, and mark on the long seatstay the location of the top of the short seatstay. The frame builder should cut the long seatstay off at this mark. If necessary, the frame builder should touch up the top ends of the seatstays with the bench grinder or file so that the seatstays are within a millimeter in length. The bench grinder can be used to correct the angle of the cuts if they are not perpendicular to the long axis of the stays. If the frame builder did not purchase seatstay caps with vent holes, he should drill vent holes on the inner surface of the seatstays approximately two inches below the top (Chapter 5).

Figure 8-25: *The frame builder marks the top of the seatstay cap plug on the seatstay. He will cut off the seatstay at this mark.*

To determine the orientation of the seatstay cap on the seatstay, the builder places one of the seatstays in the dropout, places the seatstay cap into the cut end of the seatstay by friction, and lies the cap against the ST-TT lug. The builder rotates the seatstay cap upon the seatstay until the backs of the cap lies as flat as possible upon the ST-TT lug. When he has achieved the desired orientation, the frame builder should mark a guideline that extends from the seatstay cap onto the seatstay (Figure 8-26). The builder should repeat the process with the opposite seatstay and cap. To prevent placing the wrong cap on the wrong stay, which would result in an poor orientation, the frame builder should mark a small "L" on the left cap and stay.

Figures 8-26: *Guidelines that extend from the seatstay caps onto the stays allow the frame builder correctly orient the cap prior to brazing.*

Prior to brazing, the frame builder needs to clean off all oil, debris, dirt, and oxides from the seatstays and seatstay caps. However, the frame builder should leave a small trace of the guidelines on the caps and stays so that he can return the cap to the proper orientation. Once clean, the builder should flux the plug, insert the plug in the stay using the guidelines to orient the cap, and flux the exterior of the stay and cap. When brazing, the builder should point the flame at the cap and make sure that the silver alloy binds to both the cap and the stay (Figure 8-27). In the absence of vent holes, expanding gases will cause the caps to move out of place during brazing.

Figure 8-27: *Brazing the seatstay caps onto the seatstays. The frame builder should use plenty of flux and point the torch at the cap.*

Finishing the Rear Triangle

Prior to brazing the seatstays in place, the frame builder needs to thoroughly clean the articulating surfaces of the partial dropouts on the seatstay and chainstay subassemblies as well as the backs of the seatstay caps and the sides of the ST-TT lugs. After applying flux, the builder places the articulating end of the seatstays in the drops and secures them with a C-clamp. Brake cable and vice grips can secure the seatstay caps against the ST-TT lug (Figure 8-28). The frame builder should make sure that the left and right seatstays form the same angle relative to the top tube using a protractor or angle finder if necessary.

Figure 8-28: *Brake cable and vice grips secure the tops of the seatstays (top), and C-clamps secure the bottom (bottom).*

The seatstay caps and ST-TT lug are relatively heavy pieces of metal compared to other parts of the frame. When brazing, the frame builder will have to use a large flame, moving it constantly to evenly heat up both the caps and the side of the lug. The builder wants to draw silver underneath the cap, in the space between the cap and lug, placing the rod at the top of the cap and watching it emerge from the bottom. Once the undersurface of the cap is brazed in place, the builder should close the valve regulator slightly, decreasing the size of the flame. The builder should lay down a fillet of silver along the edges of the cap, filing the small gaps between the flat underside of the cap and the convex curve of the lug.

When the caps are brazed onto the lugs, the builder should remove the two C-clamps and braze the bottom of the stays into the dropouts. The frame builder should make sure that silver alloy penetrates the entire articulating surfaces of both pieces of the dropout and should be careful not to draw out any silver from the seatstay and chainstay dropout sockets. Any gaps between the dropout and partial drop out should be completely filled with silver. With the rear triangle finished, the builder should cool and clean the frame.

Chapter 9: Small Braze-Ons

In general, small braze-ons such as the brake bridge, stay stiffeners, and cable stops are much easier to prepare and braze than the front and rear triangle. However, to produce a functional bicycle frame, the frame builder must approach small braze-ons with due diligence and avoid rushing through the remainder of the assembly.

The Brake Bridge

The brake bridge serves two functions; this structure provides a mount for u-type caliper brakes and stiffens the rear triangle. If the frame builder wishes to mount cantilever brakes, v-brakes, or is making a track bike or fixie with no brakes at all, he can use left-over seat stay scraps to build a seat stay stiffener in place of a brake bridge. The methods used to prepare a seat stay stiffener and brake bridge are similar. Stiffeners are discussed in more detail later on.

To correctly mount a brake bridge, the frame builder needs to use the u-brake he wishes to mount on his frame to draw guidelines. He should put the wheel in the dropouts, and he should adjust his u-brake so that the brake pads lie on the middle of their mounts on the calipers. This conservative estimate allows the frame builder a little lee-way in the event he mounts the brake bridge too high or too low. To estimate the location of the bridge, the builder should hold the brake in one hand and squeeze the caliper so that the brake pads touch each side of the rim, emulating the braking action. With his other hand, he should mark on the seatstays the corresponding location of the caliper's mounting bolt (Figure 9-1). These marks represent the desired location of the brake bridge. The builder should measure the distance between the stays to the nearest millimeter at these marks, and use an angle finder to determine the angle of the brake bridge, which lies parallel to the ground, relative to the seatstays (Figure 9-2).

Figure 9-1: *The frame builder pinches the calipers against the wheel and draws small guidelines where the mounting bolt lies relative to the seatstays.*

Figure 9-2: *The frame builder can use calipers or a tape measure to determine the distance between the seatstays at the future location of the brake bridge (Top). An angle finder is used to determine the angle of the brake bridge relative to the seatstays (bottom).*

Preparation of the brake bridge can be a bit tricky. Tubemiter.exe generally does not work well as a mitering tool because most brake bridges have tapering cross sectional diameters and non-uniform wall thicknesses. The frame builder will have to cut and miter the brake bridge through a combination of intuition and trial and error.

The frame builder should examine the bridge for the small holes that are used to vent water or to mount fenders. These holes, if present, should point downward when the bridge is brazed in place. If the brake caliper mounting holes are different sizes, the larger hole faces the seat tube. Once the frame builder has oriented his brake bridge, he should draw two guidelines along the rear face of the bridge at a distance from one another that corresponds to the measured distance between the two seatstays (Figure 9-3). Of course, the midpoint of these two guidelines should correspond to the caliper mounting hole. About 4 millimeters outside each guideline (toward the future location of the seatstays) the frame builder should draw another guideline. The orientation of these new guidelines should approximate the angle of the seatstays relative to the brake bridge. The frame builder should cut along these slanted guidelines, and the resulting structure should be somewhat trapezoidal in shape with the top surface of the brake bridge shorter than the bottom.

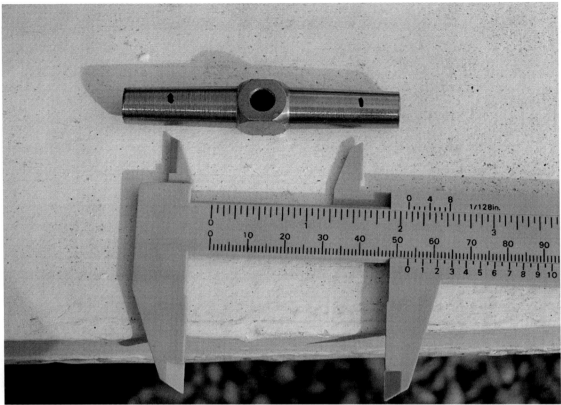

Figure 9-3: *On the brake bridge, the frame builder marks guidelines corresponding to the distance between the seatstays. The frame builder will need to cut off excess steel a few millimeters outside these marks.*

The frame builder should use a half round file, rat-tailed file, or rotary tool with small grinding bit to create concavities along the top and bottom edges of the brake bridge. After this blind mitering attempt, the builder should put the bridge in the stays, inspect the two joints for gaps, and revise his miters. He should grind or file the portions of the miter that touch the stays. The frame builder should repeat this process multiple times. With each mitering iteration, a larger portion of the miter should contact the stays until the brake bridge fits in the desired location with little or no gaps. The better the miters, the less likely the brazes of the brake bridge will fail.

After appropriately cleaning and fluxing the seatstays and brake bridge, the builder should place the frame with the dropouts pointing toward the sky, clamping the down tube in the vice (Figure 9-4). The brake bridge is placed between the stays so that the bridge is perpendicular to the plane of the front triangle and parallel to the ground. Gravity and the trapezoidal structure of the bridge should hold the structure in place during brazing. When brazing each joint, the frame builder should make sure that silver bonds to both the brake bridge and the stay.

Figure 9-4: *By placing the frame in the vice in this orientation, the frame builder can use gravity to keep the brake bridge in place during brazing.*

Stay Stiffeners

Stay stiffeners stiffen the seatstays and chainstays, making the bicycle ride less flimsily and more efficiently. Stiffeners also reduce sheering and peeling forces on the bottom bracket shell, seatstays, and dropouts, prolonging the life of the frame. Stiffeners are not mandatory but are highly recommended.

A frame with a brake bridge does not need a seatstay stiffener because the bridge serves this function. If the frame builder is building a bicycle with brake bosses for cantilever or V-brakes, he may elect to build a seatstay stiffener instead of a brake bridge.

Building a seatstay stiffener is similar to preparing and brazing a brake bridge. Scraps of seatstay that were previously cut off during the preparation of subassemblies make excellent seatstay and chainstay stiffeners. Furthermore, because seatstays scraps are generally cut off beyond the taper, they tend to have uniform wall thickness and outer diameter. The builder can, therefore, use tubemiter.exe to grind in a precise miter.

For seatstay stiffeners, the builder will want to mark on the stays a location for placement of the stiffener that allows for adequate tire clearance. He will need to determine the distance between the stays and the angle between the stay and the stiffener using the same method described above for the brake bridge (Figure 9-2). When he has these measurements, he should place two scraps of seatstay together side by side on a level surface and draw a straight guideline using a method similar for the TT and DT guidelines (Figure 7-1). The surface with the guideline will be bottom of the stiffener. The builder should place two marks on the guideline at a distance from one another equal to the measured distance between the stays. The frame builder should enter the appropriate data into tubemiter.exe and print out two copies of the template. The center of a template is aligned with the intersection of the guideline and distance mark, and the frame builder should grind in a miter. He repeats the process at the opposite end of the stiffener. After cleaning and fluxing, the frame builder places the frame in the vice so the dropouts point skyward (similar to Figure 9-4), and he brazes in the stiffener. Unlike for a brake bridge, filling in gaps between the stays and stiffer with silver fillets is less of an issue because the builder is able to make precise miters.

Making a chainstay stiffener is almost identical to a seatstay stiffener. The frame builder needs to find a location along the chainstay that allows for adequate tire clearance, find the correct angle and stay-to-stay distance, and braze the chainstay stiffener in with the dropouts pointing skyward. The only difference from the seatstay-stiffener method occurs if the builder must place the chainstay stiffener along an ovalized section of the chainstays. In this instance, the frame builder will not be able to use tubemiter.exe and will have to grind in an approximate miter using the iterative method described for brake bridge preparation. This miter will likely leave gaps between the stays and stiffener that the builder will have to fill in with silver fillets.

Cable Stops

Cable stops provide an anchor for cable housing and are essential for the proper function of shifter and brake cables. Generally, cable stops are cylindrical or bullet shaped, have a slot along the long axis, a large opening for the cable housing, and a small opening for the cable (Figure 4-3). The builder can make a simple jig with a hose clamp and a small section of narrow tube or rod made from steel or copper. Brass tubes or rods should not be used because they have a lower melting temperature than copper and steel and can melt or warp during brazing. The builder should place two bends in the rod or tube to make a type of hook (Figure 9-5). The builder should change the shape of the cross section of the bent end through crushing or filing so that the end fits into the slot of the cable stop.

Figure 9-5: *The frame builder can make a jig for small braze-ons such as cable stops with a hose clamp and a small copper or steel tube or rod bent into the shape of a hook.*

The frame builder will need to prepare the cable stop for brazing. He should place the stop securely in the vice grips so that the slotted top surface faces the angle between the jaws. Using the bench grinder, the builder should grind along the long axis of the face opposite the slot, producing a flat surface two to three millimeters in width.

The builder should clean and flux the cable stop and a section of top tube approximately two to three inches from the point of the TT-HT lug. The builder should place the stop on the top tube with the flat surface facing downward and the larger opening facing the back of the head tube. He should place the hooked end of the bent rod or tube in the slot, and secure the other end against the top tube with the hose clamp (Figure 9-6).

Figure 9-6: *The improvised jig holds the cable stop in place during brazing. The frame builder should make sure the large and small openings of the cable stop are oriented in the correct direction.*

The builder should braze the stop in place, using a small flame with low heat output. When the flux turns clear, he should place the brazing rod at the side of the stop, making sure the silver alloy bonds to both the stop and the top tube. He can either pull the silver under the stop, or manually place silver along both sides.

Assuming the frame builder wants standard cable routing for a road bike, with the shifter cables running along the down tube, he should repeat the preparation and brazing process for cable stops two more times. Another cable stop should be placed on the TT two to three inches from the point of the ST-TT lug so that the large opening faces the rear of the bike. A third cable stop should be placed on the underside of the drive-side chainstay approximately two inches from the dropout with the large opening facing the derailleur hanger. If the builder wishes to route cables in a "non-standard" way, such as for TT routed shifter cables, he will need to figure out the location and orientation of each cable stop, an intuitive task.

Shift Lever Bosses

Shift lever bosses provide an anchor for old school down tube shift levers or for barrel adjustors for the more modern STI levers. If the builder knows he will never use down tube shifters, he can braze on cable stops on the down tube in place of shift lever bosses.

The bases of most shift lever bosses are curved to match the contour of the down tube (Figure 4-3). This curve, if present, means the frame builder does not have to do any preparation other than cleaning and fluxing the boss and down tube. A curve that does not completely match the contours of the down tube is of little consequence because the joint between the boss and the tube experiences low stresses. The builder can simply fill any gaps between the two pieces with silver.

The frame builder should secure the seat tube in the vice, placing the frame on its side. Using a protractor on the seat tube and top tube, the frame builder should adjust the orientation of the frame until the plane of the front triangle is parallel to the ground (by gravity). The builder should place the clean, fluxed shift lever boss on the side of the down tube two to three inches from the DT-HT lug. The boss should be oriented so that the axis of the lever mounting hardware protrudes perpendicular to the plane of the front triangle (Figure 9-7). The builder should secure the boss with the braze-on mounting jig, placing the hook of the jig through the hole in the boss. He should braze the boss in place, drawing silver deep to the boss from back to front or side to side. In the event the frame builder accidently brazes the hooked end of the jig onto the down tube through the hole in the boss, he can unclamp the jig and secure the boss to the down tube with the hose clamp, making sure the clamp does not touch any silver brazing alloy. He can heat the boss, melting some of the filler alloy until he can pull off the jig hook with pliers or vice grips. He should allow the boss and frame to cool before attempting to remove the clamp.

Figure 9-7: *The frame builder should orient the shift lever boss so that the mounting hardware of the boss lies perpendicular to the plane of the front triangle.*

For the shift lever boss that goes on the opposite side of the frame, the builder should flip the frame over in the vice, re-orienting the frame with a protractor until the frame is parallel to the ground. He should place the second clean, fluxed boss on the down tube. By looking at the frame from its bottom, he can align the second boss with the first boss along the down tube (Figure 9-8). By looking at the frame from the front, he can align the second boss so that the mounting hardware of the two bosses line up with one another. When appropriately aligned, the builder should jig and braze the second boss.

Figure 9-8: *By looking at the frame from its bottom, the frame builder can align the second shift lever boss with the first one along the down tube. By looking at the frame from the front, the builder can make sure the mounting hardware of the two bosses line up with one another.*

Brake Bosses

Frames built for cantilever or V-brakes require a brake boss on each seat stay in place of a brake bridge. A builder can build a frame with both brake bosses and a brake bridge if the rider wishes to periodically change his braking method. Brake bosses are similar in structure to shift lever bosses and often require no special preparation. A single cantilever or V-brake has two calipers, one for the right side and one for the left. The builder should place one of the two calipers on a brake boss and align the pad of the caliper against the rim and the boss against the seat stay. He should mark the location of the boss upon the stay with a marker. After cleaning and fluxing the boss and the stay, the builder should place the frame in the vice so that the seat stays run parallel to the ground. At the mark of the seatstay, the builder should use his braze-on jig to secure the boss through the brake mounting hole with the mounting hardware of the boss oriented perpendicular to the ground. When brazing, the silver alloy should bond to both the stay and the boss. After completing the first boss, the builder should braze on the second, making sure the two bosses are well oriented and aligned.

Water Bottle Bosses

Water bottle bosses provide an anchor for the attachment of a water bottle cage to the frame. If the rider plans on never mounting a water bottle cage, then water bottle bosses are not necessary. Most water bottle bosses have a thick cross section at one end and a thin cross section at the other (Figure 4-3). The thin end is paced through holes drilled into the down tube and the thick end anchors the cage.

The frame builder should place the water bottle cage on the guideline on the top surface of the down tube. The cage should open toward the head tube and the rear of the cage should be placed towards the rear of the frame, approximately one third of the distance from the seat tube to the head tube. The builder should hold the cage with his non-dominant hand and trace the mounting holes of the cage upon the down tube with a marker (Figure 9-9).

Figure 9-9: *To make guide marks for the water bottle bosses, the builder places the water bottle cage on the center of the top surface of the down tube and traces the mounting holes onto the down tube with a marker.*

The builder should peen and drill small hole through each of the two marks following the method described in Chapter 5 (Figures 5-9 and 5-10). The builder should enlarge the hole with a larger drill bit or the small grinding bit of a rotary tool until the thin end (but not the thick end) of the water bottle boss can pass through the hole (Figure 9-10).

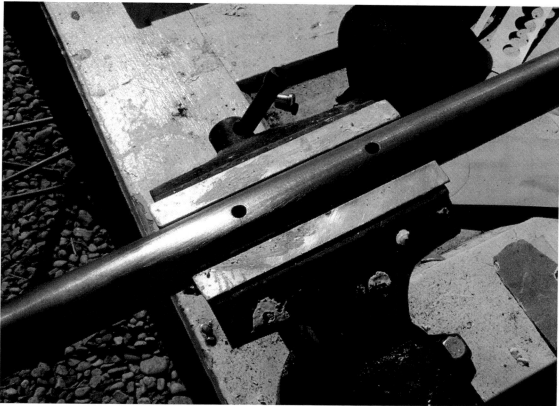

Figure 9-10: *The frame builder should peen and drill at the guide marks for the water bottle bosses and enlarge the hole until the bosses fit.*

The builder should clean and flux the down tube and water bottle bosses. He should place the bosses in the holes thick ends up so that the faces of the bosses lie flush with the down tube. Using a small flame, the frame builder can braze the bosses in place, making sure silver bonds to both the down tube and the entire circumference of each boss (Figure 9-11). He should be careful not to get filler alloy onto the threads of either boss. If he builder wishes to mount more than one water bottle cage, he can repeat the process on the front surface of the seat tube.

Figure 9-11: *Water bottle bosses brazed in place. Brazing alloy must bond to both the down tube and the bosses.*

Mounting Hardware for Shifter Cable Guides

If the frame builder acquired a BB shell with cable guides, then he does not have to worry about mounting any additional hardware. Otherwise, he should buy a small plastic cable guide from a bicycle shop and place the guide on the undersurface of the BB shell so that the guides point in the correct location. The guide for the rear shifter should point straight down the right chainstay, and the guide for the front shifter should be centered between the two chainstays (Figure 9-12). The builder should trace one of the mounting holes of the guide onto the BB shell with a marker.

Figure 9-12: *Proper location of a plastic shifter cable guide on the undersurface of the BB shell.*

The builder should acquire a T-nut that matches the hole-size of the cable guide (Figure 9-13). He should place one edge of the T-nut in the vice and use vice grips or pliers to bend the base of the T-nut so that the base roughly matches the contours of the BB shell. He should clean and flux the BB shell and T-nut and braze the T-nut in the correct location making sure filler alloy bonds to both the nut and the shell.

(As an alternative to a T-nut and plastic cable guide, the builder can acquire a steel cable guide and braze it directly to the BB shell. Generally, steel and plastic cable guides are oriented similarly [Figure 9-12]).

Figure 9-13: *The frame builder should acquire a T-nut that fits the hole of the plastic cable guide. The builder should bend the base of the T-nut so that it roughly matches the contour of the BB shell.*

Chapter 10: Finishing Touches

At this point in the build, the frame builder has finished all brazing. Tasks that remain include cutting off excess tubing, building a functional seat post clamp, cleaning, and painting the frame.

Head Tube, Final Cut

The frame builder should place the middle of the head tube in a vice. Using a hacksaw, he should remove the bulk of head tube that protrudes upward beyond the HT-TT lug (Figure 10-1). The builder should use a bench grinder to grind off excess heat tube below the HT-DT lug and above the TT-HT lug to within 1 mm of the lug rings. He should not worry about grinding the tube flush with the ring because he will have the head tube faced and reamed later on (discussed below).

Figure 10-1: *The frame builder cuts off excess head tube with a hacksaw.*

Finishing the Seat Tube

The builder should cut off excess seat tube that protrudes above the ST-TT lug. If the top of the ST-TT lug is very flat and lies in a single plane, he should use a rotary tool or bench grinder to grind excess tube to within 1mm of the top of the lug and

126

have the top of the lug faced (discussed below). If the top of the ST-TT lug is an ornate curve that does not lie in a single plane, the builder will have to use the bench grinder and rotary tool to grind the tube down flush with the top of the lug creating a nice smooth curve. If the lug was brazed correctly, the builder should be able to see a nice, uninterrupted ring of silver between the lug and tube.

To make a functional seat post clamp, the builder should move the frame, placing the seat tube or ST-TT lug in the clamp so that the dropouts point toward the sky. The builder should peen the center of the back surface of the ST-TT lug ¼ to ½" below the binding bolt eyes and drill a stress relief hold at least 1/8" in diameter (Figure 10-2). The builder should use a rotary tool with a reinforced cutting disk to cut a slot down the midline of the lug from the top of the lug down to the stress relief hole. The builder should make multiple passes with the cutting bit until the width of the slot is two to three times the thickness of the cutting disc (Figure 10-3). The builder should use a file or rotary tool with a grinding bit to clean up and smooth the edges of the slot and stress relief hole.

Figure 10-2: *Drilling a stress relief hole to turn the ST-TT lug into an effective seat post binding clamp.*

Figure 10-3: *The builder should cut a slot from the top of the lug down to the stress relief hole.*

Final Clean Up

The proprietor of the bicycle shop where the builder takes his frame to be faced and reamed will be more impressed with a clean shiny frame than a frame caked with flux, rust, and grime. The builder should thoroughly scrub his frame, using metal brushes, steel wool, sand paper, and toilet bowl cleaner until all surfaces are bright and shiny. He can hide tool marks left by files or cutting and grinding bits by sanding over them twice; once with coarse sand paper (150 grit or below) and once with medium grit paper (300 grit or above). Deep tool marks are best hidden under a thick coat or paint because excess sanding can leave steel walls thin and weak. The builder should pour toilet bowl cleaner into the inside of the tubes, scrubbing them out with a wire brush or pipe cleaner. When clean, the builder should thoroughly rinse down his frame with water and dry it as soon as possible with an old towel or clean rags to prevent the build up of rust. The builder should spray down the inside of the tubes with an oil aerosol such as WD-40® or Bicycle Frame Saver® to prevent future corrosion. If the builder lives in a humid area and will not be able to paint his frame for several days, he should wipe down the outside of the frame with an oily rag.

Reaming and Facing

The precision cutting tools needed to face and ream tubes and chase the threads of the bottom bracket shell are very expensive and generally out of the financial reach of the first time builder. (Actually, Ceeway Bicycle Building Supplies does offer some value reaming, facing, and chasing tools, but I only recommend them for frame builders who know they will build several more frames in the future). Most bicycle shops can face, chase, and ream a frame for $25 to $50.

The most available seat post diameter is 27.2mm, and I recommend the first time builder ask the shop tech to ream out his seat tube to this size. The builder should not worry if the internal diameter (tube width minus twice the wall thickness) of the non-butted end of his seat tube was greater than 27.2mm prior to frame building. Distortion of the seat tube commonly occurs during brazing of the ST-TT lug and during the cutting and drilling process used to prepare the seat post clamp, so sections of the seat tube will likely be less than 27.2mm. In the event the shop tech states that he cut out very little tube during the reaming process, the builder can make a shim to place between the seat post and seat tube by cutting apart an empty beer can. If the ST-TT lug has a flat top surface, the builder should ask the shop tech to face the top of the lug.

The builder should ask the shop tech to face the head tube so that the head tube lies flush with the rings of the HT-TT and HT-DT lug. The builder should also ask the shop tech to ream out the head tube so that he can insert the appropriately sized headset cups. A 31.7 or 31.8mm diameter head tube accommodates a headset for a 1" steering tube, and a 36mm head tube accommodates a headset for a 1 1/8" steering tube.

The builder should ask the shop tech to chase the threads of the BB shell. During frame construction, brazing alloy often bonds to the threads. Sometimes small lips from the chainstays protrude beyond the contours of the BB shell. Both of these problems prevent the insertion of a bottom bracket cartridge without stripping the threads of the shell or cartridge. Chasing the threads corrects these flaws. Facing the sides of the BB shell that face outwards so that the edges are smooth is really not necessary.

The Rattle Can Paint Job

The term "rattle can" applies to spray paint available in canisters that rattle when shaken. Most spray paint that comes in disposable cans chips and scratches very easily and is not very durable. One exception is Dupli Color® brand engine enamel. I find this brand goes on relatively smoothly and resists chipping and scratching better than any other rattle can spray paint. I am not sure if other brand engine enamel paints are as durable. Dupli Color® brand paint is generally not available at hardware stores but can be found at automotive supply stores.

If the builder wishes to paint his frame himself, he should acquire string or wire, one can of engine enamel gray primer, and two canisters of the desired engine enamel final color. After thoroughly cleaning the frame, the builder should mask the inside of the bottom bracket shell, head tube, seat tube, and the cable stops with masking tape. The builder can suspend the frame at waist height, looping the wire or string through the head tube and derailleur hanger. The frame should lie on its side, and the frame builder can place his finger in the seat tube to flip the frame over when necessary.

Detailed directions for spray painting are written on the outside of the spray cans. In short, the builder should apply three coats of primer, with a ten-minute gap between each coat. The builder should flip the frame over midway during each coat. The builder should allow seven days for the primer enamel to cure and then dry sand the primer with 400 to 800 grit sandpaper. The builder should be careful not to sand down to bare metal, and should wipe down the frame with a clean damp rag.

When spray painting the final color, the builder should use smooth even strokes. If the builder points the nozzle at a single point for a prolonged period, the paint will likely run or bleb at that location. Fortunately, most runs and blebs smooth out as the enamel cures. If the builder jerks the can or moves the spray can too rapidly, he will create an aerosol cloud. Small aerosol droplets of paint will adhere to the frame and the resulting paint job will have a gritty texture.

The builder should use approximately one and a half cans of paint for the final color, three or four coats with a ten-minute gap between each coat. Generally, multiple thin coats create a better final appearance than fewer thick coats. I do not recommend clear coating over the final color. In the event the builder needs to rebraze part of his frame (because of frame breakage or other reasons), the builder will need to sand or brush off the paint at the affected area and reapply paint after the repair is finished. A clear coat will complicate matching the texture of the paint of the repaired area to the remainder of the frame.

After the final coat has cured for seven days, the frame builder can wet sand the frame. The builder should use a soap water solution and 1500 grit sandpaper, dipping the sandpaper into the solution frequently. Blebs or runs may require dry sanding with a coarser grade (300 grit) prior to wet sanding. After wet sanding, the builder should wipe down the frame with a clean damp rag. The builder can wax the frame with a high quality automotive body polish such as Nu Finish®. Generally, waxing makes smooth shiny areas of paint appear shinier but makes coarse flat paint appear flatter.

The Professional Paint Job

Investing in an expensive professional ($100 plus) paint job can be a waste of money if the first time builder does not first test the integrity of all brazed joints. In the event the frame breaks, the builder will need to strip away the paint to re-clean, re-flux, and re-braze the broken joint.

The first time builder can test his frame in several ways. He can take his frame to a more experienced builder or an experienced brazier to inspect his brazed joints. This expert can give the builder feedback, telling him if any of the joints look weak and need to be re-brazed. If the expert gives the first time builder a passing grade, he can proceed with an expensive paint job, confident he is not wasting his money.

If an experienced brazier or frame builder is not available, an alternative for the builder is a cheap clear coat. The naked bare brushed look is popular for frames among cycling enthusiasts these days. Of course, the builder will need to remove all traces of dirt and oil prior to painting. The builder can brush the frame with a circular wire brush bit on the end of a drill to create a brushed appearance. The builder can hang the frame from a tree and paint it with an acrylic enamel clear coat. Dupli Color® brand automotive paint works well. The builder should strictly follow the directions on the spray can, keeping the nozzle the correct distance from the frame to prevent globs and runs and applying multiple thin coats several minutes apart. I recommend the builder use about 1 ½ cans of paint. Any less will result in voids and rust. Sanding the clear coat after it dries is optional. If performed the builder will need to use very fine grit (800 or above) sandpaper.

After the enamel cures, the builder should build up his clear-coated frame and ride it hard (but within its intended purposes) for about three months, inspecting all joints periodically. If a joint brakes (and the rider survives) the builder can strip away clear coat around the broken joint with a circular wire bush, clean, reflux, and re-braze the broken joint. The builder can reapply clear coat and resume riding his frame. If, after several months and hundreds of miles, all joints appear intact, the builder can pay for a professional paint job if desired. He may need to pay somebody to sandblast the frame first, which typically costs between $20 and $30.

I do not recommend the first time builder powder coat his frame. In the event of frame breakage and the need for re-brazing, powder coat paint is extremely difficult and expensive to remove. Where I live, many sandblasters simply refuse to sandblast a powder coat away.

Automotive enamel paint is durable and available in hundreds of colors. Some automobile painting businesses will paint a bicycle frame. Custom bicycle frame painting businesses also exist and usually advertise online. I do not recommend the first time builder pay more than $150 for a paint job.

I recommend the builder incorporate the lugs into the aesthetic of the frame, rather than hiding the lugs with a single solid color paint job. A common two-color theme for a lugged frame is to paint the lugs and bottom brackets one color and the tubes another (Figure 10-4). Another common motif is to use one color for the potions of the head tube and seat tube that lie intermediate to their corresponding lugs and another color for the remainder of the frame. The possibilities are endless.

Figure 10-4: *Finished frame that has been mitered, brazed, cleaned, reamed, chased, faced, and painted two colors.*

Chapter 11: Afterward

On the trail and in town, people often ask me about my bicycle. They are usually both impressed and perplexed; impressed that I put in the time to learn frame building by myself and perplexed as to why I would even bother in the first place.

Explaining how to build a frame is relatively straightforward. (I just wrote a book about it). Explaining why someone should build a frame is more difficult. I got into frame building for several reasons. Sometimes, I find myself disillusioned with some of the major players in the bicycle industry. Some of the larger bicycle manufacturers ship jobs overseas but do not seem to want to pass the savings onto the consumers. Some of the bicycle frames made in China and Taiwan cost thousands of dollars, which really irritates me. I also feel some of the "latest and greatest innovations" are neither late nor great. Some are simply rip-offs of designs made decades ago that never caught on. Others go obsolete long before the technologies they were built to replace. Don't get me wrong. I feel many of the smaller domestic frame and component manufacturers still make fantastic stuff, but these companies are confined to smaller high-end niche markets within the cycling industry. My hope is that this manual will help create many new frame builders and that eventually most communities will have local frame builders to compete with companies that make mid-level mass produced imported frames.

Currently we live in a consumer society with massed-produced goods that are made as cheaply as possible and built to be replaced and not repaired. Many people have become intimidated by the idea of actually building something "from scratch" like a bicycle frame. They often wonder why they should put forth the time and effort to actually make something themselves when they can buy it from a store. Once they actually put forth the time and effort to create something with their hands, however, they often find the whole process extremely rewarding. I know I did.

Another local frame builder I know once described frame building as "glorified plumbing" and there is a fair amount of truth to this statement. The science is straightforward, and I do my best to describe the science completely but concisely in the preceding pages of this manual. The truth is any motivated individual can build a quality bicycle frame. There is no witchcraft involved.

Unlike the science, the art of frame building, which is what results in truly awe-inspiring aesthetics, takes a life time to master. Hopefully the user of this manual found that his first frame build was frustrating enough to provide just the right amount of challenge and not so frustrating as to put him off of frame building forever. If he enjoyed the process, he should consider building a second frame, trying techniques I discourage in this book such as bending tubes and lugs and maybe investing in additional tools and resources.

Chapter 12: Recommended Reading and Other References

Books

1. Paterek, Tim (2004). *The Paterek Manual For Bicycle Framebuilders, Shop Edition.* Portland, USA: Tim Paterek.
2. Cain, Tubal (2008). *Soldering and Brazing, Workshop Practice Series Number 9.* Norfolk, UK: Special Interest Model Books.
3. Slone, Eugene A. (1995). *Slone's Complete Book of Bicycling.* New York, USA: Simon & Schuster.
4. Heine, Jan et al. (2005). *The Golden Age of Handbuilt Bicycles.* Seattle, USA: Vintage Bicycle Press.
5. Finch, Richard (2007). *Welder's Handbook.* Berkley, USA: Berkley Publishing Group.

Online Frame Building Supplies

1. Nova Cycles Supply (2009). Available at URL: http://www.novacycles.com/catalog/. Last accessed 15 June 2009.
2. Bikelugs.com (2009). Available at URL: http://www.bikelugs.com/. Last accessed 15 June 2009.
3. Henry James Bicycles (2009). Available at URL: http://www.henryjames.com/. Last accessed 15 June 2009.
4. Ceeway Bike Building Supplies (2009). Available at URL: http://www.ceeway.com/. Last accessed 15 June 2009.
5. Fairing Industrial Inc. (2009). Available at URL: http://www.fairing.com/. Last accessed 15 June 2009.
6. Bringheli Frames-Tools & Jigs (2009). Available at URL: http://www.bringheli.com/. Last accessed 15 June 2009.

Tool Retailers

1. Sears, Roebuck and Co. (2009). Available at URL: http://www.sears.com/. Last accessed 15 June 2009.
2. Lowe's Home Improvement (2009). Available at URL: http://www.lowes.com/lowes/lkn?action=home. Last accessed 15 June 2009.
3. The Home Depot (2009). Available at URL: http://www.homedepot.com/. Last accessed 15 June 2009.
4. Ace Hardware (2009). Available at URL: http://www.acehardware.com/home/index.jsp. Last accessed 15 June 2009.
5. Harbor Freight Tools (2009). Available at URL: http://www.harborfreight.com/. Last accessed 15 June 2009.

Brazing Supplies

1. Air Gas, Gas, Welding, Safety Supply (2009). Available at URL: http://www.airgas.com/. Last accessed 15 June 2009.
2. Brazage Silver Brazing Products (2009). Cycle Design Group. Available at URL: http://www.cycledesign.org/brazage.htm. Last accessed 15 June 2009
3. High Silver Brazing Alloys (2009). Harris Products Group. Available at URL: http://www.harrisproductsgroup.com/consumables/alloys.asp?id=30. Last accessed 15 June 2009.

Online Frame Building Resources

1. Giles Puckett's Programs (2009). Available at URL: http://moz.geek.nz/mozbike/giles.html. Last accessed 15 June 2009.
2. Little Fish Hobby Stuff (2009). Available at URL: http://www.littlefishbicycles.com/. Last accessed 15 June 2009.
3. Silver Brazing Lugged Bicycle Joint with MAPP Gas (2009). Youtube. Available at URL: http://www.youtube.com/watch?v=u94WsKf6JRo. Last accessed 15 June 2009.
4. Bicycle Frame Building Part 2 (2009). Youtube. Available at URL: http://www.youtube.com/watch?v=gMtS8IpWeaU. Last accessed 15 June 2009.
5. How to Miter a Tube (2009). Youtube. Available at URL: http://www.youtube.com/watch?v=42nP42sbhEI. Last accessed 12 August 2009.

Frame Painting and Finishing Resources

1. Premium General Purpose Paints (2009). Dupli Color®. Available at URL: http://www.duplicolor.com/products/premium.html. Last accessed 15 June 2009.
2. Weigle Frame Saver® (2009). Velo Orange. http://www.velo-orange.com/wefrsa.html. Last accessed 15 June 2009.
3. Mike's Bikes Custom Frame Painting Service (Unofficial Name, 2009). Fort Collins, Colorado. Email: dirtmcguirk@gmail.com.
4. Custom Paint Options, Vicious Cycles (2009). Available at URL: http://www.viciouscycles.com/paint.php3. Last accessed 15 June 2009.
5. Decal Zone (2009). Available at URL: http://www.decalzone.com/. Last accessed 15 June 2009.
6. Nu Finish® (2009). Available at URL: http://nufinish.com/. Last accessed 12 August 2009.
7. DIY Bicycle 29er Frame Paint Job with Rattle Can Paint (2009). Youtube. Available at URL: http://www.youtube.com/watch?v=uQ26Nw9xM0w. Last accessed 12 August 2009.

3750034

Made in the USA